THE AMERICAN NEGRO

HIS HISTORY AND LITERATURE

WORKING
WITH THE HANDS

Booker T. Washington

ARNO PRESS and THE NEW YORK TIMES
NEW YORK 1969

Introduction copyright © 1969 by Arno Press, Inc.

*

Library of Congress Catalog Card No. 76–92241

*

Reprinted from a copy in the collection of the
Wisconsin State Historical Society Library

*

Manufactured in the United States of America

General Editor
WILLIAM LOREN KATZ

Booker T. Washington remains a misunderstood caricature to the larger American reading public in spite of nearly two decades of revision and reevaluation of his place in history. He has been like a celebrity whose public image grew to be a distortion of his own personality. His book, *Working With the Hands,* is an expression of the public Washington who rose from slavery to become a world-renowned educator of his people. He subtitled it *A Sequel to "Up From Slavery" Covering the Author's Experiences in Industrial Training at Tuskegee.*

Missing is what Louis R. Harlan has called "the secret life" of Washington: the politician, the manipulator of white philanthropists, the "power" who controlled the destinies of other Negroes, a covert battler for lost civil rights. Until recently, this side of Washington has lain obscured in his own personal papers or exposed only in a few anti-Washington black journals such as William Monroe Trotter's Boston *Guardian* and W. E. B. Du Bois's *Horizon.*

For most of Washington's life, and for nearly a third of a century after his death, he was regarded in simple terms: first a living, then a canonized, saintly stereotype. During his lifetime some Negroes knew the accommodating, self-effacing educator—the "Moses of his people." Others knew him as the despotic "Wizard of Tuskegee," an authoritarian who could brook no opposition in the black world, and who used his power to build an empire of industrial training schools at the expense of academic education. Still others, among them a number of white men, knew him as a political inside-dopester and wire-puller. In this latter category were the managers of patronage for the Republican Party. It was they, not the rhetoreticians of the party, who dealt with Negroes. James S. Clarkson, Theodore Roosevelt's assistant postmaster general, and Frank Hitchcock, Taft's postmaster general, both came to know the political Washington. A few selected white businessmen, such as W. H. Baldwin, Jr. of the Long Island Railroad, were also permitted to see through the accommodationist Washington who told Uncle Tom stories while extracting philanthropic funds from rich men's open and yielding checkbooks.[1]

During his lifetime it was important to Washington that he be known as merely the humble ex-slave who helped his people to rise to the level of yeomen and bourgeoisie. Thus, except for his critics, few writings of his contemporaries revealed the many facets of Washington. For example, in his laudatory capsule biography, Roscoe Conkling Bruce, a Tuskegee staff member, emphasized Washington's cleanliness and punctuality. He wrote of the youthful days spent mourning "Mars Billy," his master's son who was killed in the Civil War, and of the time the Wizard pawned his watch in order to raise funds with which to make bricks.[2]

Whites praised or condemned in Washington what they admired or resented in all Negroes. They exalted his "great commonness" and enjoyed reading *Working With the Hands, The Man Farthest Down,* and his other works which confirmed their beliefs that the Negro's progress rested on self-help and white tutelage. White men such as John Daniels in his 1914 study of black Boston, readily praised Washington's accommodation and "common sense," by which Negroes could be uplifted. Two years later, B. F. Riley, a sympathetic white, praised Washington's educational philosophy and his meticulously kept records of lynchings. In his biography of Washington he recorded only one political adventure, the famous dinner at the White House with Theodore Roosevelt at which the two men discussed patronage in the South. Riley ignored its implications, dismissed it as an accident of scheduling, and accepted the myth that it was merely a casual, unplanned luncheon. Alfred Holt Stone, a paternalistic white man from the Mississippi delta, found comfort in Washington's doctrine which held that "the Negro is at his best in the Southern states." He praised Washington for declaring that "relations of kindliness and friendship between the Southern white man and the Negro afford the latter 'a protection and guarantee of his rights that will be more potent . . . than . . . any outside power can confer.' "[3]

In Washington's lifetime and after his death the black community, needing white philanthropy and knowing of

Washington's influence, rarely criticized his vision of southern-black-yeoman-as-Horatio Alger. For example, early in the twentieth century only a few northern Negroes joined with W. E. B. Du Bois in signing an open letter attacking Washington's optimistic speeches to European audiences. The critics wrote: "Mr. Washington's large financial responsibilities have made him dependent on the rich charitable public and . . . he has for years been compelled to tell, not the whole truth, but that part of which certain powerful interests in America wish to appear as the whole truth."[4] Washington rarely replied publicly to such attacks, preferring to offer homilies such as: "As a rule, the place to criticize the South . . . is in the South—not in Boston."[5]

From the very beginnings of his impact on the political scene Washington preferred to conceal his maneuvering behind the image created by his ghost writers. And since few men during Washington's lifetime knew the full extent of political dealing, and those who owed him gratitude for jobs awarded by Roosevelt or Taft could hardly acknowledge their debt, the activist Washington remained obscure behind a self-imposed curtain of pious autobiographies and press releases. Presidents Roosevelt and Taft, their patronage bosses, the many black consuls, customs collectors, land officers, collectors of public monies, recorders of deeds, internal revenue collectors, and the whites who owed their judicial robes or marshal's badges to Washington, all maintained the stony silence which Washington felt was necessary to hold his power and to further the work of Tuskegee Institute.

His influence on political life extended through much of the administrations of Roosevelt and Taft. From the day in the fall of 1901 when Roosevelt first wrote: "When are you coming North? I must see you as soon as possible. I want to talk over the question of possible appointments in the South exactly on the lines of our last conversation," Washington's influence among whites grew and his power over Negroes increased. His secretary reported of the Negroes in the nation's capital: "The colored brethren here are scared. They don't know what to expect, and the word has passed, they say, that you are the 'Warwick' so far as they are concerned."[6]

Soon hundreds of Negroes and whites wrote plaintive letters asking for jobs, favors, recommendations, and endorsements. Occasionally he used his position to increase the wealth of Tuskegee Institute, as when he used the influence of ex-Senator Henry W. Blair to lobby for acquisition of prime mineral land for the school. Baldwin of the Long Island Railroad thought that "through your personal influence in Washington . . . you can get the authorities to turn over to you the best land owned by the Government."[7]

However, in order to hold such power and live in the midst of the white South, Washington developed a shrewd cautiousness that allowed his enemies to believe he abhorred politics and that he favored only industrial education for Negroes. This is not to say there was only a covert Washington. He openly fought against disfranchisement in Georgia, Alabama, and Louisiana. Just as vigorously, he protested against discrimination in education, railroad facilities, and economic opportunity. And privately, he could write to his friend, T. Thomas Fortune, that: "We must keep hammering away at these fellows until a fellow can feel that he can go to Harvard or Yale and . . . still go into the South or elsewhere and do business just as a white man does. There is no need why every colored man who graduates . . . should go to teaching or preaching."[8]

Unfortunately for the Negro world, Washington's political career was short lived. His little band of Republican politicians, Charles W. Anderson of New York, Ralph Tyler of Ohio, and the other black office holders, contributed to Taft's successful campaign for the presidency in 1908, but in a few months much of the black power ended. Washington claimed that he "rewrote" much of the racial parts of Taft's nomination acceptance speech "otherwise [Taft] would have made a great bungle of it." But even though Taft wrote to Washington that he intended to consult with him on racial matters, Washington knew that the old days of playing politics were over.[9]

As the Republican Party veered away from racial liberalism, whatever reputation for political power that Washington had was gradually silted over. His activities in civil rights cases were buried in his personal papers. And what remained to be shaped into an iconography for future generations was the myth of the humble ex-slave who rose to be the educator of his people.

After Washington's death in 1915, a veil closed over this corner of his biography. Emmett J. Scott, Washington's private secretary, presided over the closing by co-authoring, with the genteel white magazine editor, Lyman Abbott, a biography of the Wizard.[10] Whenever the biography mentioned Washington's power, it was to minimize or deny it. Few writers thereafter deviated from the stereotype of Washington, the unctuous flatterer, the Uncle Tom whose every word and deed was a concession to the powerful whites upon whom he depended for his own power.

Two generations of historians and journalists forgot the full range of Washington's work. White and black, radical and conservative, northerner and southerner, all perceived Washington through the same mythic haze, and agreed on the essential traits of the man. They differed only in their approval or condemnation of what they saw.

U.S. Communist leader William Z. Foster described Washington's famous Atlanta Compromise speech of 1895 as "obsequious" and cynically compared Washington to the labor "misleader," Samuel Gompers. Another Marxist, Oliver C. Cox, blamed Washington for naively aiding whites in keeping the Negro "proletarianized," although he admitted that any alternative would have led blacks to "an unproductive, unexpressed, sullen hate" of the counterrevolutionary South and the apathetic North.[11]

Popular white American opinion accepted the humble model left by Scott's early reverential biography. Textbooks in American history either ignored Washington or presented Scott's official version of the man. At best he was a "Moses of his people," urging them to be pious, industrious, materialistic, acquisitive, and to seek only the rudiments of education and become good mechanics, artisans, and farmers. This figure usually emerged following some catch phrase such as "the greatest Negro leader of his time."[12] Such historical judgments allowed racists to embrace him as a perfect model of Negro leadership from which more recent black leaders had sharply and wrongly deviated. As late as 1961 Carlton Putnam in his book, *Race and Reason,* took this position.[13] A popular account of Washington's life in the *Reader's Digest* followed Putnam's reasoning, but suggestive of its paternalistic viewpoint, referred to him only as "Booker" or "Professor Washington."[14]

Often, for the same reasons that whites praised him, black writers viciously attacked Washington. Yet even when they were critical of him, writers such as Benjamin Brawley, Roi Ottley, and J. Saunders Redding invariably treated him kindly in their versions of his rise from slavery to Tuskegee. A generation of black writers often attacked what Washington may have intended as a temporary retreat or a passing phenomenon, but which they judged to be a permanent philosophical position. Rayford Logan, for example, concluded that he "definitely renounced social equality." Roi Ottley attributed to Washington minimal power over only a small group of political hacks, but granted that Washington may have done the best he could in view of the fact that changes in Negro status in many respects were dependent on southern whites.[15]

W. E. B. Du Bois's early opposition to Washington provided the origins of a school which made the Wizard the center of a conscious plot to manipulate Negroes for his own gain. Herbert Aptheker believed this to be Washington's motive for thwarting the "Negro liberation movement," by which he meant the abortive Niagara Movement, whose members eventually drifted into the NAACP. Redding used Du Bois's term, "The Tuskegee machine," to describe Washington's machinations which he attributed to "latent egomania."[16]

Of all the black critics after Washington's death, yet before the deposit of his papers in the Library of Congress, only Horace Mann Bond captured the dichotomy of the man. Bond saw that although Washington "embodied the survival elements of the Negro race in an environment hostile to its ultimate objectives," he was forced to choose "indirection" as the only tactic which would allow survival. Bond based his criticism of Washington more on assessing mistakes than imputing ulterior motives. He felt that Washington misjudged the good will of southern Bourbons, failed to take fully into account the triumph of the poor white in southern politics, and exaggerated the values of the bucolic life in an industrial society.[17]

Bond's position continued to prevail even after a generation of scholars began to revise historical judgments based on an examination of the Washington manuscripts in the Library of Congress. First came C. Vann Woodward's impressionistic but perceptive chapter in his *Origins of the New South, 1877–1913,* to be followed by seminal articles by August Meier, Samuel Spencer's biography, and Louis R. Harlan's article on Washington "and the White Man's Burden," the forerunner of a forthcoming biography.[18] These historians have attempted to present a rounded picture of Washington in the context of his time. This new Washington emerges as no hero. His victories were small and his positions equivocal, but all of the recent historians have given him his due as at least a covert militant. Herbert J. Storing, for example, pointed out that he led Negroes into citizenship while Indian leaders chose the slow death of non-assimilation. Meier speaks of his "direct attack" on the American race system though acting "surreptitiously." Both Elliott Rudwick and Francis L. Broderick, biographers of Dr. Du Bois, agreed with Kelly Miller's hesitant praise that Washington "would not disclaim, in distinct terms, a single plank in the platform of Douglass," yet Broderick emphasized the Wizard's "soft speech and accommodating manner." Rudwick pointed out how closely the philosophies of the two leaders meshed.[19]

Generally, popular accounts such as those by Arna Bontemps, Charles Silberman, Louis Lomax, and Benjamin Quarles have agreed with the monographic interpretations. One recent writer, Harold Cruse, even suggested the deep thread of black economic nationalism that ran through Washington's thinking, and in effect, called for a further reevaluation of the man. Only Lerone Bennett, Jr. intemperately attacked Washington with a parody: "Work. Save. Pray. Clean up and paint up. Buy land and don't antagonize the white folk with fuzzy talk about social and political equality."[20]

As black militancy grows and makes gains, Washington's achievement, rhetoric and tactics may seem increasingly irrelevant. As Emma Lou Thornbrough has recently observed: "Washington was a man very much in step with his times, and the heroes of history are likely to be men who are ahead of their times." Yet the historian would be guilty of shameless "presentism" were he to dismiss Washington on this ground. The Wizard's failures are more related to his own times. He misjudged the racial commitment of the Republican Party. He had a misplaced trust in the southern Bourbons, while unable to reach a rapprochement with the poor whites. He never realistically faced the powerful unions, mass production techniques, and urbanization that radically changed the America into which he had been born. The Negro yeomen and sharecroppers whom he intended to make into petit bourgeois property holders impatiently moved cityward looking for more immediate gratification in northern factories. Even his contribution to the defeat of a "Lily White" movement in the Republican Party was not permanent, for the Republicans by the 1920's turned to no national Negro spokesman for advice on patronage and racial matters. His achievement consisted of a desperate holding action while Negroes moved to a new northern habitat, a new political party, a campaign to win civil rights through the courts, and finally a program of direct action.

The gradual reemergence of the many-sided Washington is reason enough for reprinting *Working With the Hands*. But it should be clear beforehand to the reader that *only* Washington, the educator of Tuskegee, will show forth from the pages. All of the ingredients of the old Washington stereotype are present. In the beginning he argues the need for industrial education both from a vantage of American and African experience. So often, he claims, Negroes saw freedom as merely an abandonment of the need to work. And in Africa, he insists, there had never been any social or economic imperative to work. He staunchly demands that his students reject the city, even to the point of having no pictures of urban scenes on the walls. The effete, academically trained he calls "hothouse" plants, as opposed to the hard working, practical Tuskegee graduate. He lovingly invokes a feeling for tools, even claiming that to write a sentence with pen in hand is more satisfying than dictating to a secretary (thus ignoring the vast amount of his own books and articles that were ghost-written). The academic subjects are useful, he insists, but merely for their practical value; language as a communicator, not a set of rules; mathematics as a computing tool, not an esoteric system. His advice to mothers is: "Go to town on Thursday instead of Saturday. Buy no more than you need. Stay in town no longer than necessary." And he enjoins the race "to stop throwing away our time and money on Saturdays by standing around towns, drinking and disgracing ourselves." There is only a bare hint of the "Tuskegee machine" in the proprietary descriptions of Tuskegee-inspired work in Vorhees, Mt. Meigs, Snow Hill, Utica, Christianburg and other industrial schools, and of the work in Togo where the "natives" fared better after having been taught Tuskegee methods.

The lesson is clear: to be black and fail to adopt the teaching of head, hand and heart in the Tuskegee style is to go the way of Haiti, with its scholarly traditions in a setting of abject poverty.[21] Washington wanted none of that for his people.

Thomas R. Cripps
PROFESSOR OF HISTORY
MORGAN STATE COLLEGE

[1] Hundreds of letters in the Booker T. Washington Papers (hereafter BTWP), Library of Congress, express this side of Washington's life. See for example, Booker T. Washington to Whitefield McKinlay, February 18, 1902; Booker T. Washington to Theodore Roosevelt, October 3, 1902; Booker T. Washington to James S. Clarkson, October 7, 1901; Booker T. Washington to Emmett J. Scott, July 22, 1908; Ralph Tyler to Scott, July 21, 1908; Booker T. Washington to William Howard Taft, November 30, 1908; W. H. Baldwin, Jr., to Booker T. Washington, February 18, 1899.

[2] American Unitarian Association, *From Servitude to Service* (Boston, 1905), pp. 83–85.

[3] John Daniels, *In Freedom's Birthplace: The Story of Boston Negroes* (Boston, 1914), pp. 415–16; B. F. Riley, *The Life Times of Booker T. Washington* (London, 1916), pp. 128–30; Alfred Holt Stone, *Studies in the American Race Problem* (New York, 1908), pp. 164–251; Ray Stannard Baker wrote of his "great commonness" in *Following the Color Line* (New York, 1908), p. 220. For an example of a white man who nagged Washington for being "impertinent" [sic], see W. W. Brewer to Booker T. Washington, May 9, 1898, BTWP.

[4] William Edward Burghardt Du Bois, *A Pageant in Seven Decades, 1868–1938* (Atlanta, 1938), pp. 28–29.

[5] Booker T. Washington, *Up From Slavery* (New York, 1901), p. 201.

[6] Theodore Roosevelt to Booker T. Washington, September 14, 1901; Emmett J. Scott to Booker T. Washington, October 5, 1901, BTWP.

[7] W. H. Baldwin, Jr. to Booker T. Washington, February 18, 1899, BTWP.

[8] Booker T. Washington to T. Thomas Fortune, March 1, 1899, BTWP.

[9] Booker T. Washington to Emmett J. Scott, July 22, 1908; Booker T. Washington to William Howard Taft, November 30, 1908, BTWP.

[10] Emmett J. Scott and Lyman Beecher Stowe, *Booker T. Washington: Builder of a Civilization* (Garden City, 1916).

[11] William Z. Foster, *The Negro People in America* (New York, 1954), p. 410; O. C. Cox, *Caste, Class and Race* (New York, 1948), p. 344.

[12] For examples of racial analyses of American history textbooks see Kenneth M. Stampp, et al., *The Negro in American History Textbooks* (Sacramento, 1964). For the quotation see T. Harry Williams, Richard N. Current, and Frank Freidel, *A History of the United States Since 1865* (New York, 1964, 2nd ed., rev.), p. 108.

[13] Carlton Putnam, *Race and Reason: A Yankee View* (Washington, 1961), pp. 90, 95.

[14] O. K. Armstrong, "Booker T. Washington: Apostle of Good Will," *Reader's Digest,* L (February, 1947), pp. 25–30.

[15] Benjamin Brawley, *Negro Builders and Heroes* (Chapel Hill, 1937), p. 151; Roi Ottley, *Black Odyssey* (New York, 1948), pp. 213–16; J. Saunders Redding, *They Came in Chains: Americans from Africa* (Philadelphia, 1950), pp. 195–204; Rayford Logan, *The Negro in American Life and Thought: The Nadir, 1877–1901* (New York, 1954), Chap. XIV.

[16] Herbert Aptheker, *Toward Negro Freedom* (New York, 1949), p. 103; Redding, *They Came in Chains,* p. 197.

[17] Horace Mann Bond, *Negro Education in Alabama: A Study in Cotton and Steel* (Washington, 1939), pp. 206 ff.

[18] C. Vann Woodward, *Origins of the New South, 1877–1913* (Baton Rouge, 1951), Chap. XIII; August Meier, "Booker T. Washington and the Negro Press: With Special Reference to the *Colored American Magazine,*" *Journal of Negro History,* XXXVIII (1953), pp. 67–90; "Booker T. Washington and the Rise of the NAACP," *The Crisis,* LXI (1954), pp. 69–76, 117–123; "Toward a Reinterpretation of Booker T. Washington," *Journal of Southern History,* XXIII (1957), pp. 220–27; Louis R. Harlan, "Booker T. Washington and the White Man's Burden," *American Historical Review,* LXXI (1966), pp. 441–67; Samuel R. Spencer, Jr., *Booker T. Washington and the Negro's Place in American Life* (Boston, 1955).

[19] Herbert J. Storing, "The School of Slavery: A Reconsideration of Booker T. Washington," in Robert A. Goldwin, *One Hundred Years of Emancipation* (Chicago, 1964), pp. 80–88; Meier, "Toward a Reinterpretation of Washington," p. 226; Francis L. Broderick, *W. E. B. Du Bois: Negro Leader in a Time of Crisis* (Stanford, 1959), pp. 65–6; Elliott Rudwick, *W. E. B. Du Bois: A Study in Minority Group Leadership* (Philadelphia, 1960), pp. 63–66.

[20] Harold Cruse, *The Crisis of the Negro Intellectual* (Cleveland, 1967) *passim;* Leone Bennett, Jr., *Before the Mayflower: A History of the Negro in America, 1609–1962* (Chicago, 1962), p. 237.

[21] In addition to the writings previously cited, two other important sources of bibliography are Hugh Hawkins, *Booker T. Washington and His Critics* (Boston, 1963), and E. L. Thornbrough, ed., *Booker T. Washington* (Englewood Cliffs, 1969).

WORKING WITH THE HANDS

OTHER BOOKS

BY

THE SAME AUTHOR

CHARACTER BUILDING

UP FROM SLAVERY

WORKING
WITH THE HANDS

BEING A SEQUEL TO "UP FROM SLAVERY"
COVERING THE AUTHOR'S
EXPERIENCES IN INDUSTRIAL
TRAINING AT TUSKEGEE

By

BOOKER T. WASHINGTON

Illustrated from photographs by Frances Benjamin Johnston

NEW YORK
DOUBLEDAY, PAGE & COMPANY
1904

PREFACE

For several years I have been receiving requests, from many parts of the United States, and from foreign countries as well, for some detailed information concerning the value of industrial training and the methods employed to develop it. This little volume is the result, in part, of an attempt to answer these queries. Two proven facts need emphasis here:

First: Mere hand training, without thorough moral, religious, and mental education, counts for very little. The hands, the head, and the heart together, as the essential elements of educational need, should be so correlated that one may be made to help the others. At the Tuskegee Institute we find constantly that we can make our industrial work assist in the academic training, and *vice versa.*

Second: The effort to make an industry pay its way should not be made the aim of first importance. The teaching should be most emphasised. Our policy at Tuskegee is to make an industry pay its way if possible, but at the same time not to sacrifice the training to mere economic gain. Those who undertake such endeavour with the expectation of getting much money out of an industry, will find themselves disappointed, unless they realise that the institution must be, all the time, working. upon raw material. At Tuskegee, for example, when a student is trained to the point of efficiency where he can construct a first-class wagon, we do not keep him there to build more vehicles, but send him out into the world to exert his trained influence and capabilities in lifting others to his level, and we begin our work with the raw material all over again.

I shall be more than repaid if these chapters will serve the purpose of helping forward the cause of education, even though their aid be remote and indirect.

CONTENTS

LIST OF ILLUSTRATIONS

WORKING WITH THE HANDS

WORKING WITH THE HANDS

CHAPTER I

MORAL VALUES OF HAND WORK

THE worth of work with the hands as an up-lifting power in real education was first brought home to me with striking emphasis when I was a student at the Hampton Normal and Agricultural Institute, which was at that time under the direction of the late General S. C. Armstrong. But I recall with interest an experience, earlier than my Hampton training, along similar lines of enlightenment, which came to me when I was a child. Soon after I was made free by the proclamation of Abraham Lincoln, there came the new opportunity to attend a public school at my home town in West Virginia. When the teacher said that the chief purpose of education was to enable one to speak and write the English language correctly, the statement found lodgment in my mind and stayed there. While at the time I could not put my thoughts into words clearly enough to express instinctive disagreement with my teacher, this definition did not seem adequate, it grated harshly

3

upon my young ears, and I had reasons for feeling that education ought to do more for a boy than merely to teach him to read and write. While this scheme of education was being held up before me, my mother was living in abject poverty, lacking the commonest necessaries of life, and working day and night to give me a chance to go to school for two or three months of the year. And my foremost aim in going to school was to learn ways and means by which I might make life more endurable, and if possible even attractive, for my mother.

There were several boys of our neighbourhood who had superior school advantages, and who, in more than one instance, had reached the point where they were called "educated," which meant that they could write and talk correctly. But their parents were not far removed from the conditions in which my mother was living, and I could not help wondering whether this kind of education alone was fitted to help me in the immediate needs of relieving the hard times at home. This idea, however, ran counter to the current of widespread opinion among my people. Young as I was, I had come to have the feeling that to be a free boy meant, to a considerable extent, freedom from work with the hands, and that this new status applied especially to the educated boy.

Just after the Civil War the Negro lad was strongly influenced by two beliefs; one, that freedom from slavery brought with it freedom from hard work, the other that education of the head would bring even more sweeping emancipation from work with the hands. It is fair to add that the Negro was not directly responsible for either of these ideas, but they warped his views nevertheless, and held sway over the masses of the young generation. I had felt and observed these things, and further, as a child in Virginia, had naturally noted that young white boys whose fathers held slaves did not often work with their hands.

Not long after I had begun to think of these new conditions and their results, viewing them as seriously as could be expected of an ignorant boy, an event of my working life left important influences in its wake. There lived a little way from my mother's cabin a woman of wealth, who had lived many years in the South, although she had been born and educated in Vermont. She had a high respect for manual labour, showing actively her appreciation of the dignity of honest work well done, and, notwithstanding her own position and culture, she was not ashamed to use her hands. In the neighbourhood, this lady was reputed to be exceedingly hard to please in the performance of any sort of work on her place, and among the village boys she was called a "hard person to get along with."

As I remember, at least half a dozen boys had been successively chosen to live with her, but their residence in service had been consistently short-lived. I think a week was about the average period, in spite of the widely advertised fact that the household had the redeeming reputation of always providing good things to eat. In addition to pies and cakes, which boys in a community like ours seldom saw in their own cabin homes, the orchards around the house bore heavy yields of the finest fruits, yet such extraordinary inducements as these could not hold the boys, who one by one returned to the village with the same story, that the lady of the mansion was too strict and too hard to please.

After a long record of these mutual disappointments, my mother told me that my turn had come, as the rich and exacting personage had sent to ask me to come and live with her, with the promise of five dollars a month in wages. After a long and serious talk with my mother I decided to make the effort to serve this woman, although the tidings of so many failures filled me with foreboding. A few days later, with my clothes made as presentable as possible, and with my heart thumping in fear and anxiety, I reported for duty.

I had heard so much about Mrs. Ruffner, her wealth, her fine house, and her luxurious surroundings, overshadowed by her appalling severity and exacting discipline, that I trembled with a terror which I shall not try to describe at the thought of facing her. My life had been lived in a cabin, and I was now to try to toil in what looked to me like a grand mansion, an enchanted palace filled with alarms. But I got a grip on all the courage in my scanty stock, and braced myself to endure the ordeal with all possible fortitude.

The meeting was not at all what I had expected. Mrs. Ruffner talked to me in the kindliest way, and her frank and positive manner was tempered with a rehearsal of the difficulties encountered with the boys who had preceded me, how and why they had failed to please, and what was expected of them and of me. I saw that it would be my fault if I failed to understand my duties, as she explained them in detail. I would be expected to keep my body clean and my clothes neat, and cleanliness was to be the motto in all my work. She said that all things could be done best by system, and she expected it of me, and that the exact truth at all times, regardless of consequences, was one of the first laws of her household—a law whose violation could never be overlooked.

I remember, too, that she placed special emphasis upon the law of promptness, and said that excuses and explanations could never be taken in the place of results. At the time, this seemed to me a pretty stern program to live up to, and I was fighting a sense of discouragement when, toward the end of the interview, she told me that if I were able to please her she would permit me to attend school at night during the winter. This suggestion so stimulated my ambition that it went a long way toward clinching the decision to make the effort of my life to satisfy my employer and to break all records for length of service in her household.

My first task, as I remember it, was to cut the grass around the house, and then to give the grounds a thorough "cleaning up." In those days there were no lawn-mowers, and I had to go down on my knees and cut much of the grass with a little hand-scythe. I soon found that my employer not only wished the grass cut, but also demanded that it be trimmed smooth and even. Any one who has tried to mow a lawn with a dull hand-scythe or sickle can realise the difficulties which beset this labour. I am not ashamed to say that I did not succeed in giving satisfaction the first, or even the second or third time, but at last I made the turf in that yard look as smooth and velvety as if I had been over it with the most improved pattern of lawn-mower. With this achievement my sense of pride and satisfaction began to stir itself and to become a perceptible incentive. I found, however, that cutting the grass was not the whole task. Every weed, tuft of dead grass, bit of paper, or scrap of dirt of any kind must be removed, nor did I succeed at the first attempt in pleasing my employer. Many times, when tired and hot with trying to put this yard in order, I was heartsick and discouraged and almost determined to run away and go home to my mother.

But I kept at it, and after a few days, as the result of my efforts under the strict oversight of my mistress, we could take pleasure in looking upon a yard where the grass was green, and almost perfect in its smoothness, where the flower beds were trimly kept, the edges of the walks clean cut, and where there was nothing to mar the well-ordered appearance.

When I saw and realised that all this was a creation of my own hands, my whole nature began to change. I felt a self-respect, an encouragement, and a satisfaction that I had never before enjoyed or thought possible. Above all else, I had acquired a new confidence in my ability actually to do things and to do them well. And more than this, I found myself, through this experience, getting rid of the idea which had gradually become a part of me, that the head meant everything and the hands little in working endeavour, and that only to labour with the mind was honourable while to toil with the hands was unworthy and even disgraceful. With this vital growth of realisation there came the warm and hearty commendation of the good woman who had given me what I now consider my first chance to get in touch with the real things of life.

When I recall this experience, I know that then

and there my mind was awakened and strengthened. As I began to reap satisfaction from the works of my hands, I found myself planning over night how to gain success in the next day's efforts. I would try to picture the yard as I meant it to look when completed, and laid awake nights trying to decide upon the prettiest curves for the flower beds and the proper width of the walks. I was soon far more absorbed in this work than in filling in my leisure time seeking mischief with the village boys.

I remained in this family for several years, and the longer I was employed there the more satisfaction I got out of my work. Instead of fearing the woman whom the other boys had found so formidable, I learned to think of her and to regard her now (for she still lives) as one of my greatest teachers. Later, whether working in the coal mines or at the salt furnaces, I learned to find the same kind of satisfaction in everything I did for a livelihood. If while sweeping or dusting a room, or weeding a bed of flowers or vegetables, there remained the least imperfection, I was unhappy, and felt that I was guilty of dishonesty until the flaw in my work had been removed.

While I have never wished to underestimate the awakening power of purely mental training, I believe that this visible, tangible contact with nature gave me inspirations and ambitions which could not have come in any other way. I favour the most thorough mental training and the highest development of mind, but I want to see these linked with the common things of the universal life about our doors.

It was this experience in using my hands that led me, in spite of all the difficulties in the way, to go to the Hampton Institute, where I had learned that pupils could have not only their minds educated, but their hands trained. When I entered the Hampton Institute few industries were taught there, but these had to do with the fundamentals of every-day life. The hand work began with the duties which lay directly in the path of the student. We were taught to make our own beds, to clean our rooms, to take care of the recitation rooms, and to keep the grounds in order. Then came lessons in raising our food on the farm and the proper methods of cooking and serving it in the school. The instruction in iron and wood-work in the earlier years of the institution was mostly in making and repairing the farming implements and in helping to maintain the buildings.

While much of this work may seem rudimentary, it had great educational value. How well I remember the feeling of stimulus and satisfaction inspired by the sight of a perfectly made bed, the pillows placed always at the right angle, and the edges of the sheets turned over according to rules of neatness and system. The work of the farm had a similar kind of influence upon my views of relative values in education. I soon learned that there was a great difference between studying about things and studying the things themselves, between book instruction and the illumination of practical experience.

This chain of experiences, whose links I have tried to indicate, served as a preparation for the work of training the head, the heart, and the hands which I was to undertake later at the Tuskegee Normal and Industrial Institute in Alabama. When I went to Alabama to begin this work, I spent some time in visiting towns and country districts in order to learn the real conditions and needs of the people. It was my ambition to make the little school which I was about to found a real service in enriching the life of the most lowly and unfortunate. With this end in view, I not only visited the schools, churches, and farms of the people, but slept in their one-roomed cabins and ate at their tables their fare of corn-bread and fried pork.

Often while making these visits, both in the towns and in the plantation districts, I found young men and women who had acquired considerable education, but it seemed to be limited to memorising certain rules in grammar and arithmetic. Some of them had studied both the classic and modern languages, and I discovered students who could solve problems in arithmetic and algebra which I could not master.

Yet I could not escape the conviction that the more abstract these problems were, and the further they were removed from the life the people were then living, or were to live, the more stress seemed to be placed upon them.   One of the saddest features was to find here and there instances of those who had studied what was called "art" or "instrumental music," in other words "the elegant accomplishments," but who were living in houses where there was no sign of beauty or system.   There was not the slightest indication that this art or these accomplishments had had or ever would have any influence upon the life in the homes of these people.

Indeed, it did not seem to have occurred to them that such things ought to have any relation to their every-day life.   I found young men who could wrestle successfully with the toughest problems in "compound interest or banking" or "foreign exchange," but who had never thought of trying to figure out why their fathers lost money on every bale of cotton raised, and why they were continually mortgaging their crops and falling deeper into debt. I talked with girls who could locate on the map accurately the Alps and the Andes, but who had no idea of the proper position of the knives and forks on the dinner table.   I found those who remembered that bananas were grown in certain South and Central American countries, but to whom it had never occurred that they might be a nourishing and appetising food for their breakfast tables.

In a country where pigs, chickens, ducks, geese, berries, peaches, plums, vegetables, nuts, and other wholesome foods could be produced with little effort, school teachers were eating salt pork from Chicago and canned chicken and tomatoes sent from Omaha. While the countryside abounded in all manner of beautiful shrubbery and fragrant flowers, few of these ever found their way into the houses or upon the dinner tables. While in many instances the people had always lived in the country, and would continue to do so, what few text-books I saw in their cabins were full of pictures and reading matter relating to city life. In these text-books I saw pictures of great office buildings, ships, street-cars, warehouses, but not a single picture of a farm scene, a spreading apple-tree, a field of grass or corn, a flock of sheep, or a herd of cows.

CHAPTER II

Training for Conditions

The preliminary investigation of certain phases of the life of the people of my race led me to make a more thorough study of their needs in order that I might have more light on the problem of what the Tuskegee Institute could do to help them. Before beginning work at Tuskegee I had felt that too often in educational missionary effort the temptation was to try to force each individual into a certain mould, regardless of the condition and needs of the subject or of the ends sought. It seemed to me a mistake to try to fit people for conditions which may have been successful in communities a thousand miles away, or in times centuries remote, without paying attention to the actual life and needs of those living in the shadow of the institution and for whom its educational machinery must labour.

In the beginning of my work, when I thought it necessary to investigate at closer range the history and environment of the people around us, it soon became evident that this data was a valuable basis for the undertaking at Tuskegee. For it was demonstrated that we were about to take a share in the burden of educating a race which had had little or no need for labour in its native land, before being brought to America—a race which had never known voluntary incentives to toil.

The tropical climate had been generous to the inhabitant of Africa and had supplied him without effort with the few things needful for the support of the body. I had cause to recall the story of a native who went to sleep on his back in the morning under a banana tree with his mouth open, confident that before noon a providential banana would fall into his mouth. While the African had little occasion to work with his hands in the land of his nativity, by the end of his period of slavery in this country he had undergone two hundred and fifty years of the severest labour. Therefore, many friends of the race argued that the American Negro, of all people, ought to be released from further hand-training, especially while in school. Others said that the Negro had been worked for centuries, and now that the race was free there ought to be a change.

At Tuskegee we replied that it was true that the race had been worked in slavery, but the great lesson which the race needed to learn in freedom was *to work*. We said that as a slave the Negro was worked; as a freeman he must learn to work. There is a vast difference between working and being worked. Being worked means degradation; working

BREAKING UP NEW GROUND WITH AN EIGHT-OX TEAM

means civilisation. This was the difference which our institution wished chiefly to emphasise. We argued that during the days of slavery labour was forced out of the Negro, and he had acquired, for this reason, a dislike for work. The whole machinery of slavery was not apt to beget the spirit of love of labour.

Because these things were true we promised to try to teach our students to lift labour out of drudgery and to place it on a plane where it would become attractive, and where it would be something to be sought rather than something to be dreaded and if possible avoided.

More than this, we wanted to teach men and women to put brains into the labour of the hand, and to show that it was possible for one with the best mental training to work with the hands without feeling that he was degraded. While we were considering our plans at Tuskegee, many persons argued with me, as they had done with General Armstrong years before, at Hampton, that all the Negro youth needed as education was mental and religious training, and that all else would follow of itself.

Partly in answer to this argument, we pointed to our people in the republic of Hayti, who were freed many years before emancipation came to our race in the Southern States. A large number of the leading citizens of Hayti during the long period of years had been given a most thorough mental training not only in Hayti but in France, and the Catholic Church had surrounded the population from birth with religious influences. Many Haytians had distinguished themselves in the study of philosophy and the languages, and yet the sad fact remained that Hayti did not prosper.

I wish to be entirely fair to the Haytians. Hayti exports annually from sixty to eighty million pounds of coffee and several hundred million pounds of precious woods. A French statistician says that "among the sixty countries of the globe which carry on regular commerce with France, Hayti figures in the seventeenth place. In amount of special duties received at the French Custom House upon the products imported from those sixty countries, Hayti comes in the fourth rank." It seems well to observe, then, that here is the foundation for the upbuilding of a rich and powerful country, with great natural resources. It seems all the more inexcusable that industrial conditions should be as unsatisfactory as they are.

The thoughtful and progressive men in the republics of Hayti and Santo Domingo now recognise the fact that while there has always been a demand for professional men and women of the highest type of scholarship, at the same time many of these scholars should have had such scientific and industrial education as would have brought them into direct contact with the development of the material resources of the country. They now see that their country would have been advanced far beyond its present condition, materially and morally, if a large proportion of the brightest youths had been given skilled handicrafts and had been taught the mechanical arts and practical methods of agriculture. Some of them should have been educated as civil, mining, and sanitary engineers, and others as architects and builders; and most important of all, agriculture should have been scientifically developed. If such a foundation had been laid it is probable that Hayti would now possess good public roads, streets, bridges, and railroads, and that its agricultural and mining resources would have made the country rich, prosperous, and contented.

It is a deplorable fact that one of the richest islands in natural resources in the world is compelled to import a large proportion of its food and clothing. It is actually true that many of the people of Hayti, some of them graduates of the best universities of France, content themselves with wearing clothes imported from Europe. It is also true that great quantities of canned meats and vegetables are brought from the United States, commodities which could easily be produced at their very doors. The Haytians claim, however, that most of the imported food is for the use of foreigners, as they, themselves, eat very little meat that is not freshly cooked. The people live almost wholly upon the primitive products of undisturbed nature, and the greater part of the harvesters and other workers are women.

I have been told, upon reliable authority, that the majority of the educated persons in the island take up the professions, and that because there is almost no industrial development of the country, the lawyer, naturally, finds himself without clients, and he, in common with others of the educated classes, spends much of his time in writing poetry, in discussing subjects in abstract science, or embroiling his country in revolutions.

In recent years I have received most urgent appeals from both Hayti and Santo Domingo for advice and assistance in the direction of educating industrial and scientific leaders. The best friends of Hayti and Santo Domingo now realise that tremendous mistakes have been made. They see that if the people had been taught in the beginning of their freedom that all forms of idleness were disgraceful and that all forms of labour, whether with the head or with the hand, were honourable, the country to-day would not be in such stress of poverty. They would have fewer revolutions, because the people would have industries to occupy their time, their thoughts, and their energies. I ought to add that, in such deficiencies as these, Hayti is perhaps not worse off than some South American republics which have made the same mistakes.

The situation in these countries which have overlooked the value of industrial training remind me of a story told by the late Henry W. Grady about a country funeral in Georgia. The grave was dug in the midst of a pine forest, but the pine coffin that held the body was brought from Cincinnati. Hickory and other hard woods grew in abundance nearby, but the wagon on which the coffin was drawn came from South Bend, Indiana, and the mule that drew the wagon came from Missouri. Valuable minerals were close to the cemetery, but the shovels and picks used in digging the grave came from Pittsburg, and their handles from Baltimore. The shoes in which the dead man was buried came from Lynn, Massachusetts, his coat and trousers from New York, his shirt from Lowell, Massachusetts, and his collar and tie from Philadelphia. The only things supplied by the county, with its wealth of natural resources, was the corpse and the hole in the ground, and Mr. Grady added that the county probably would have imported both of these if it could have done so.

When any people, regardless of race or geographical location, have not been trained to habits of industry, have not been given skill of hand in youth, and taught to love labour, a direct result is the breeding of a worthless idle class, which spends a great deal of its time in trying to live by its wits. If a community has been educated exclusively on books and has not been trained in habits of applied industry, an unwholesome tendency to dodge honest productive labour is likely to develop. As in the case of Hayti, the people acquire a fatal fondness for wasting valuable hours in discussing politics and conspiring to overthrow the government. I have noted, too, that when the people of a community have not been taught to work intelligently with their hands, or have not learned habits of thrift and industry, they are likely to be fretting continually for fear that no one will be left to earn a living for them.

There are few more dismal and discouraging sights than the men of a community absorbed in idle gossip and political discussion. I have seen more than a dozen white men in one small town take their seats under a tree or on the shady side of the street as early as eight o'clock in the morning and talk politics until noon. Then they would go home for dinner, and return at one o'clock to spend the remainder of the day threshing out the same threadbare topics. Their greatest exertion during the whole long day would be in moving from the sunny side of the street or tree to the shady side and back again. A curious trait of such parasites is that they are always wondering why "times are hard," and why there is so little money in circulation in their communities.

An argument handed down from Reconstruction

times was once urged by many people, both
white and coloured, against industrial education.
It was to the effect that because the white South
had from the first opposed what is popularly called
"higher education" for the Negro, this must be the
only kind good for him. I remember that when I
was trying to establish the Tuskegee Institute, nearly
all the white people who talked with me on the subject took it for granted that instruction in Greek,
Latin, and modern languages would be main features
in our curriculum; and I heard no one oppose what
it was thought our course of study would embrace.
In fact, there are many white people in the South at
the present time who do not know that the dead
languages are not taught at Tuskegee.

Further proof of what I have said will be furnished
by the catalogs of the schools maintained by the
Southern States for Negro people, and managed by
Southern white people; it will be found that in
almost every instance instruction in the higher
branches is given with the consent and approval
of white officials. This was true as far back as
1880. It is not unusual to meet even at this time
Southern white people who are as emphatic in their
belief in the value of classical education as a certain
element of the coloured people themselves. But the
bulk of opinion in the South had little faith in the
efficacy of the "higher" or any other kind of education for the Negro. They were indifferent, but

did not openly oppose. Not all have been indifferent, however, for there has always been a potent element of white people in all the Southern States who have stood up openly and bravely for the education of all the people, regardless of race. This element has had considerable success thus far in shaping and leading public opinion, and I believe it will become more and more influential. This does not mean that there is as yet an equitable division of the school funds raised by common taxation.

While the education which we proposed to give at the Tuskegee Institute was not spontaneously welcomed by the white South, it was this training of the hands that furnished the first basis for anything like united and sympathetic interest and action between the two races at the South and the whites at the North and those at the South. Aside from its direct benefits to the Negro race, industrial education, in providing a common ground for understanding and coöperation between the North and South, has meant more to the South and to the cause of education than has been realised.

Many white people of the South saw in the movement to teach young Negroes the necessity and honour of work with the hands a means of leading them gradually and sensibly into their new life of freedom, without too sudden a transition from one extreme to the other. They perceived, too, that the Negroes who were master carpenters and contractors under the guidance of their owners could greatly further the development of the South if their children were not too suddenly removed from the atmosphere and occupations of their fathers, but taught to use the thing in hand as a foundation for still higher growth.   Some were far-sighted enough to see that industrial education would enable one generation to secure economic independence, and the next, on this foundation, to obtain a more abstract education, if desired.   The individual and community interest of the white people was directly appealed to by industrial education. They perceived that intelligence, coupled with skill, would add wealth, in which both races would increasingly share, to the community and to the State. While crude labour could be managed and made to some degree profitable under the methods of slavery, it could not be so utilised in a state of freedom. Almost every white man in the South was directly interested in agricultural, mechanical, or other manual labour; in the cooking and serving of food, laundering and dairying, poultry-raising, and everything related to housekeeping in general.   There was no family whose interest in intelligent and skillful nursing was not now and then quickened by the presence of a trained nurse.

Therefore there came to be growing appreciation of the fact that industrial education of the black people had a practical and vital bearing on the life of every white family in the South. There was little opportunity for such appreciation of the results of mere literary education. If a black man became a lawyer, a doctor, a minister, or an ordinary teacher, his professional duties would not ordinarily bring him in touch with the white portion of the community, but rather confine him to his own race. While professional education was not opposed by the white South as a whole, it aroused little or no interest, beyond a confused hope that it would produce a better and higher type of Negro manhood. Industrial education, however, soon recommended itself to the white South, when they saw the Negro not only studying chemistry, but its applications to agriculture, cooking, and dairying; not merely geometry and physics, but their application to blacksmithing, brickmaking, farming, and what not. A common bond at once appeared between the two races and between the North and the South.

A class of people in the South also favoured industrial education because they saw that as long as the Negro kept abreast in intelligence and skill with the same class of workmen elsewhere, the South, at present free from the grip of the trade union, would continue free from its restrictive influences. I should like to make a diversion here to call attention to the fact that official records show that within one year about one million foreigners came into the United States, yet practically none of the immigra-

CUTTING SUGAR-CANE ON THE SCHOOL'S FARM

tion went into the Southern States. The records show that in 1892 only 2,278 all told went into the States of Alabama, Arkansas, Georgia, Kentucky, Mississippi, North Carolina, South Carolina, Tennessee, and Virginia. One ship sometimes brings as many as these to New York in one trip. Foreigners avoid the South. It must be frankly recognised by the people of that section that for a long period they must depend upon the black man to do for it what the foreigner is doing for the Great West, and that they cannot hope to keep pace with the progress of people in other sections if one-third of the population is ignorant and without skill. If the South does not help the Negro up, it will be tying itself to a body of death. If by reason of his skill and knowledge one man in Iowa can produce as much corn in a season as four men can produce in Alabama, it requires little reasoning to see that Alabama will buy most of her corn from Iowa.

An instance which illustrates most interestingly the value of education that concerns itself with the common things about us, is furnished by Professor Geo. W. Carver, the Director of our Agricultural Department. For some time it has been his custom to prepare articles containing information concerning the condition of local crops, and warning the farmers against the ravages of certain diseases and insects. Some months ago a white landholder in Montgomery County asked Mr. Carver to inspect his farm. While doing so, Mr. Carver discovered traces of what he thought was a valuable mineral deposit used in making a 'certain kind of paint. The interests of the agricultural expert and the landholder at once became mutual. Mr. Carver analysed specimens of the deposits in the laboratory at Tuskegee and sent the owner a report of the analysis, with a statement of the commercial application and value of the mineral. It is an interesting fact that two previous analyses had been made by chemists who had tabulated the constituents with greatest accuracy, but failed to grasp any idea of value in the deposits. I need not go into the details of this story, except to say that a stock company, composed of some of the best white people in Alabama, has been organised, and is now preparing to build a factory for the purpose of putting the product on the market. I hardly need add that Mr. Carver has been freely consulted at every step, and that his services have been generously recognised in the organisation of the concern.

Now and then my advocacy of industrial education has been interpreted to mean that I am opposed to what is called "higher" or "more intellectual" training. This distorts my real meaning. All such training has its place and value in the development of a race. Mere training of the hand without mental and moral education would mean little for the welfare of any race. All are vital factors in a harmonious plan. But, while I do not propose that every individual should have hand training, I do say that in all my contact with men I have never met one who had learned a trade in youth and regretted it in manhood, nor have I ever seen a father or mother who was sorry that his children had been taught trades.

There is still doubt in many quarters as to the ability of the Negro, unguided, and unsupported, to hew out his own path, and put into visible, tangible, indisputable forms the products and signs of civilisation. This doubt cannot be extinguished by mere abstract arguments, no matter how ingeniously and convincingly advanced. Quietly, patiently, doggedly, through summer and winter, sunshine and shadow, by self-sacrifice, by foresight, by honesty and industry, we must re-enforce arguments with results. One farm bought, one house built, one home neatly kept, one man the largest tax-payer and depositor in the local bank, one school or church maintained, one factory running successfully, one truck-garden profitably cultivated, one patient cured by a Negro doctor, one sermon well preached, one office well filled, one life cleanly lived—these will tell more in our favour than all the abstract eloquence that can be summoned to plead our cause. Our pathway must be up through the soil, up through swamps, up through forests, up through the streams and rocks; up through commerce, education, and religion!

In my opinion we cannot begin at the top to build a race, any more than we can begin at the top to build a house. If we try to do this, we shall reap in the end the fruits of our folly.

CHAPTER III

A BATTLE AGAINST PREJUDICE

WHEN the first few students began to come to Tuskegee I faced these questions which were inspired by my personal knowledge of their lives and surroundings:

What can these young men and women find to do when they return to their homes?

What are the industries in which they and their parents have been supporting themselves?

The answers were not always to my liking, but this was not the point at issue. I had to meet a condition, not a theory. What I might have wanted them to be doing was one thing; what they were actually doing was the bed-rock upon which I hoped to lay the foundation of the work at Tuskegee.

It was known that a large majority of the students came from agricultural districts and from homes in which agriculture in some form was the mainstay of the family. I had learned that nearly eighty per cent of the population of what are commonly called the Gulf States are dependent upon agricultural resources, directly or indirectly. These facts made me resolve to attempt in downright earnest to see what the Tuskegee Institute could do for the people of my race by teaching the intelligent use of hands and brains on the farm, not by theorising, but by practical effort. The methods in vogue for getting enough out of the soil to keep body and soul together were crude in the extreme. The people themselves referred to this heart-breaking effort as "making a living." I wanted to teach them how to make more than a living.

I have little respect for the farmer who is satisfied with merely "making a living." It is hardly possible that agricultural life will become attractive and satisfactory to ambitious young men or women in the South until farming can be made as lucrative there as in other parts of the country where the farmer can be reasonably sure of being able to place something in the bank at the end of the year. For the young farmer to be contented he must be able to look forward to owning the land that he cultivates, and from which he may later derive not only all the necessities of life, but some of the comforts and conveniences. The farmer must be helped to get to the point where he can have a comfortable dwelling-house, and in it bathtubs, carpets, rugs, pictures, books, magazines, a daily paper, and a telephone. He must be helped to cherish the possibility that he and his family will have time for study and investigation, and a little

GRINDING SUGAR-CANE AT THE SCHOOL'S SUGAR-MILL

time each year for travel and recreation, and for attending lectures and concerts.

But the average farmer whom I wanted to help through the medium of the Tuskegee Institute was far from this condition. I found that most of the farmers in the Gulf States cultivated cotton. Little or nothing in the form of stock or fowls, fruits, vegetables, or grain was raised for food. In order to get the food on which man and live stock were to live while the cotton crop was being grown, a mortgage or lien had to be given upon the crop, or rather upon the expected crop, for the legal papers were usually signed months in advance of the planting of the crop.

Cotton in the South has been known for years as "the money crop." This means that it is the one product from which cash may be expected without question as soon as the crop is harvested. The result of this system has been to discourage raising anything except cotton, for the man who holds the mortgage upon the crop discourages, and in some cases prevents, the farmer from giving much of his time and strength to the growing of anything except cotton, since the money-lender is not sure that he can get his money back from any other crop.

The result of this has been that, beginning in January, the farmer had to go to the store or to the money-lender for practically all of his food during the year. The rate of interest which the farmer had to pay on his "advances" was in many cases enormous. The farmer usually got his "advances" or provisions from a storekeeper. The storekeeper in turn borrowed money from the local bank. The bank, as a general thing, borrowed from New York. By the time the money reached the farmer he had to pay in not a few cases a rate of interest which ranged from 15 to 30 per cent. If he failed to make his payment at the end of the year he was likely to be "cleaned up"—that is, everything in sight in the way of crops or live stock was taken from him. After being "cleaned up" he would either try to make another crop on the same rented farm—trusting to Providence or the weather for better luck—or else move to another farm and go in search of some one else to "run him," as the local expression describes the process. Not a few of the farmers whom I met had been "cleaned up" half a dozen times or more.

In addition to having to pay the high rate of interest for food supplies and clothing advanced, the ground rent was also to be paid. By far the greater part of the land was rented. This, of course, had a hurtful effect. Because the man who tilled the land did not own it, his main object was to get all he could out of the property and return to it as little as possible. The results were shown in the wretched cabins and surroundings. If a fence was out of repair, or the roof of the house leaked, the tenant had no personal interest in keeping up the premises, because he was always expecting to move, and he did not want to spend money upon the property of other people.

Instead of returning the cotton-seed to the ground to help enrich the soil, he sold this valuable fertiliser. The land, of course, was more impoverished each year. Ditching and terracing received little attention. The mules with which the crops were made were rented or were being bought "on time," as a rule, and the farmer did not have enough direct interest in them to encourage him to spend money in keeping them in prime condition. Besides, the food fed to the animals was not raised on the place, but had to be bought.

Another serious result of the "one-crop" system was that the farmers handled almost no cash except in the fall. To the ignorant and inexperienced men of my race this was hurtful. If by any chance they were able to pay their ground rent, and the principal and exorbitant interest charged for their "advances," and have a few dollars in cash left, the money did not remain with them long, for it came into their hands about Christmas time, when the temptation to spend it for whisky, cheap jewelry, cheap buggies, and such unprofitable articles was too strong to be resisted. Had the same value been in the hands of the farmer in the form of corn, vegetables, fruit, stock, or fowls it would have been

not only less likely to be wasted, but it would also
have been available for the farmer and his family
during the whole or the greater part of the year.

The conditions which I have described had a discouraging effect upon many people who tried to
get their living from the soil.   As numbers of them
expressed it to me, if they worked hard during the
year they came out at the end in debt, and if they
did not work they found themselves in debt anyhow.
Some went so far as to perform only sufficient work
to "make a show" of raising enough cotton on
which to get "advances" during the year, with no
thought of ridding themselves of debt or of coming
out ahead.

Notwithstanding these conditions, there were instances each year of individuals who triumphed over
all these difficulties and discouragements and came
out with considerable money or cotton to their
credit.   These men soon got to the point where they
could begin to buy their own homes.

In justice to the class of men in the South who
advance money or provisions each year to the
farmers, I ought to say that many of them deplore
the state of affairs to which I have referred as much
as any one, but with them it is simply a system of
lending money on uncertain security.   If these
advances were not made, in many instances the
farmers and their families would starve.   The
average merchant prefers to deal with the man who

owns his land and can pay cash for his goods, but the many ramifications of the mortgage system make both the farmer and the money-lender slaves to the one-crop plan. If cotton fails, or if the tenant abandons the crop before it is matured, the money-lender is bound to lose. Both with the farmer and the money-lender it has been like the old story of the man hugging the bear, each desperately anxious to find a way to get free.

From the first I was painfully conscious of the fact that I could do very little through the work of the Tuskegee Institute to help the situation, but I was determined to make an effort to do what I could. Many of my own race had been reduced to discouragement and despair. Before the school could begin its practical help I spent all the time that could be spared in going about among the people, holding meetings, and talking with individual leaders, to arouse their ambition, and inspire in them hope and confidence.

My first effort was to try to help the masses through the medium of the thing that was nearest to them, and in which they had the most vital and practical interest. I knew that if we could teach a man's son to raise forty bushels of corn on an acre of ground which had before produced but twenty bushels, and if he could be taught to raise this corn with less labour than before, we should gain the confidence and sympathy of that boy's father at once.

In this connection I have often thought that missionaries in foreign countries would make greater progress if at first more emphasis were placed upon the industrial and material side than upon the purely spiritual side of education. Almost any heathen family would, I believe, appreciate at once the difference between a shack and a comfortable house, while it might require years to make them appreciate the truths of the Bible. Through the medium of the home the heart could be reached. Not long ago I was asked by a missionary who was going into a foreign field what, in my opinion, he ought to teach the people, and how he ought to begin. I asked him what the principal occupation of the people was among whom he was going, and he replied that it was the raising of sheep. I advised him, then, to begin his missionary work by teaching the people how to raise more sheep than they were raising and better sheep, and said that I thought the people would soon decide that a man who could excel them in the raising of sheep might also excel them in the matter of religion, and that thus the foundation for effectual mission work might be laid.

The first few students of our school came largely from the farming districts. The earliest need at the Tuskegee School was food for teachers and students. I said: "Let us raise this food, and while doing so teach the students the latest and best methods of farming." At the same time we could teach them the dignity and advantages of farm life and of work with their hands. It was easy to see the reasons for doing this, and easy to resolve to do it, but I soon found that there were several stubborn and serious difficulties to be overcome. The first and perhaps the hardest of these was to conquer the idea, by no means confined to my race, that a school was a place where one was expected to do nothing but study books; where one was expected not to study things, but to study about things. Least of all did the students feel that a school was a place where one would be taught actually to *do* things. Aside from this, the students had a very general idea that work with the hands was in a large measure disgraceful, and that they wanted to get an education because education was something which was meant to enable people to live without hand work.

In addition to the objections named, I found that when I began to speak very gently and even cautiously to the students about the plan of teaching them to work on the farm, two other objections manifested themselves with more or less emphasis. One was that most of the students wanted to get out of the country into a town or a city, and the other that many of them said they were anxious to prepare themselves for some kind of professional life, and that they therefore did not need the farm work. The most serious obstacle, however, was the argument that since they and their parents for generations back had tilled the soil, they knew all there was to be known about farming, and did not need to be taught any more about it while in school.

These objections on the part of the students were reinforced by the parents of many of them. Not a few of the fathers and mothers urged that because the race had been worked for two hundred and fifty years or more, now it ought to have a chance to rest. With all of my earnestness and argument I was unable in the earlier years of the school to convert all the parents and students to my way of thinking, and for this reason many of the students went home of their own accord or were taken home by their parents. None of these things, however, turned the school aside from doing the things which we were convinced the people most needed to have done for them.

I shall always remember the day when we decided actually to begin the teaching of farming—not out of books, but by real and tangible work. In the morning I explained to the young men our need of food to eat, and the desire of the school to teach them to work with their hands. I told them that we would begin with the farm, because that was the most important need. The young men were greatly surprised when the hour came to begin work to find me present with my coat off, ready to begin digging up stumps and clearing the land. As my first request was more·in the form of an invitation than a command, I found that only a few reported for work. I soon learned, too, that these few were ashamed to have any one see them at work. After we had put in several hours of vigorous toil I noticed that their interest began to grow, because they came to realise that it was not *my* farm they were helping to cultivate, but that it belonged to the school, in which we all had a common interest. The next afternoon a larger number reported for duty. They were still shy about having any one see them at work, however, and were especially timorous at the idea of being caught in the field by the girl students.

Gradually, year by year, the difficulties which I have enumerated began to melt away, but not without constant effort and very trying embarrassments. It soon became evident that the students had practical knowledge of only one industry, and that was the cultivation of cotton in the manner in which it had been grown by their fathers for years. Another defect soon became evident, and that was that they had little idea of caring for tools or live stock. Plows, hoes, and other farming implements were left in the field where they were last used. If quitting time came when the hoe was being used in the middle of a field or at the end of a row, the tool remained there over night. Where the last plowing in the fall was done, there the plow would most likely spend the winter.   No better care than this was given to wagons or harness, and mules and horses shared this impartial neglect.

It was the custom in the earlier days of the school —as it is now—for students and teachers to assemble in the evening for prayers. After considerable ineffective effort to teach the students to put their implements away properly at night, I caused a mild sensation at evening prayers by calling the names of three students who had left their implements in the field.   I said that these three students would be excused from the room to attend to this duty, and that we would not proceed with the service until their return, and that I felt sure they would be more benefited by prayer and song after having done their work well than by leaving it poorly done.   A few lessons of this kind began to work a notable betterment in the care with which the students looked after their implements, and attended to other details of their daily round.

THE REPAIR SHOP

All of the broken furniture of the school is mended here

CHAPTER IV

Making Education Pay Its Way

I CANNOT emphasise too often the fact that my experience in building up the Tuskegee Institute has taught me year by year the value of hand work in the building of character. I have frequently found one concrete, definite example illustrating the difference between right and wrong worth more than hours of abstract lecturing on morality. I have told girls many times that a dish is either thoroughly washed and dried or it is not. If a thing is not well done, it is poorly done. Furthermore, I have taught our girls from the beginning of this school that a student who receives pay for properly attending to dishes, and does her work poorly, is guilty of two wrongs. She is guilty of falsehood and guilty of receiving money for doing something which she has not done.

This lesson taught in the kitchen, with the carelessly cleaned utensil in evidence as an illustration, has a power that is hard to resist. Just so the implement left in the field over night has many times been made to teach the same lessons—of warning against untruth and dishonesty. Leaving it there was untruthful, because the student had said by his action that he had properly performed the work of the day; it was dishonest because the school had been robbed of a portion of the value of the implement by reason of the rain and dew falling on it and causing it to rust and depreciate in value.

In the beginning our methods of instruction in farming were primitive and crude, but month by month, and year by year, steady growth encouraged our efforts. One difficulty to which I have not referred was that the land on which we began work was not the richest in the world. When attention was called by the students and others to the poor quality of the soil, I replied that poor soil was the best in which to begin the teaching of agriculture, because this would give us an opportunity to learn to make poor land rich. I told them also that if we could teach the students how to cultivate poor land profitably they would have little difficulty in making more than a living upon fairly good or rich soil.

Apart from the problems found on the school grounds, our methods were at first misunderstood by school officials in high authority throughout the country, and our aims were not appreciated by other schools established in the South for the education of my race. I remember that after I had spoken for an hour at a meeting of a State Teachers' Association, trying to explain the meaning and advantages of industrial education or hand work, a teacher arose and asked the State superintendent, who was present, a very simple question regarding the subject. The superintendent replied that he would have to refer the question to me, as the subject was one that he had never heard discussed before. It happened occasionally that students on their way to the Tuskegee Institute were asked if they were going to an "ox-driving school," the question implying, I suppose, that the main thing taught at Tuskegee was ox-driving. Our critics, however, did not know that at the time we were too poor to own oxen, and that on our little farm we had nothing in the way of draught animals except one poor blind horse which a white friend in Tuskegee had given us.

During the first year the training in agriculture on the school farm consisted of about two hours of work daily for each of the young men students, the remaining time being spent in the class rooms. The outdoor period, during the first school session, was mostly spent in grubbing up stumps, felling trees, building fences, making ditches, and in plowing the ground preparatory to planting a little crop. We had few implements with which to do this work, and most of these were borrowed. The reader will realise how hard it must have been under these conditions to make the student feel that he was acquiring new knowledge of farm life. As I recall it now, I am sure that the main thing that we were able to teach the students in those early days was that book education did not mean a divorce from work with the hands.

Gradually we were able to secure more land for farming purposes and to cultivate what we did have to better advantage. As the school grew, we learned more about the proper fertilisation of the soil, and how to use labor-saving machinery more effectively. It was surprising to note how many of the students believed that farm labour must from its very nature be hard, and that it was not quite the proper thing to use too much labour-saving machinery. Indeed, many of the white planters in certain sections of the South have until recently refused to encourage the use of much agricultural machinery, for the reason, as they stated it, that such assistance would spoil the Negro "farm hands." For some years the Tuskegee Institute did not escape this charge As our department of farming grew from month to month, I was not afraid to let it be known that I felt certain that one result of any proper system of hand training *was* to spoil, or get rid of, the ordinary "farm hand." If one will study the industrial development of the South, he will be forced to the conclusion that one of the factors that has most retarded its progress has been and is the "farm hand." This individual has too long controlled the agriculture of the South.

With few exceptions, he is ignorant and unskilled, with little conscience. He seldom owns the land which he pretends or tries to cultivate. Too often he is a person who has no permanent abiding place, and if he has one it is probably a miserable one-room cabin. The "farm hand" can be hired for from forty to sixty cents a day. In fact, I have known of cases where such men were hired for twenty-five cents a day and their board; and they were very dear help even at that price.

I believe that most of the worn-out and wasted fields, the poor stock, the run-down fences, the lost and broken farm tools and machinery, as well as the poor crops, are chargeable to the "farm hand" whom, I have been warned so many times, I must be careful not to spoil. Such a man is too ignorant to know what is going on in the world in progressive agriculture. He is without skill to such an extent that he knows almost nothing about setting up and operating labour-saving machinery. His conscience has not been trained, and hence he has little idea of giving an honest day's labour for a day's pay, and of doing unto others in matters of labour as he would have others do unto him.

It will be seen at a glance that such a worker in the soil as this cannot compete with the farmer of the Northwest, who owns the land that he cultivates, who is intelligent, and who uses the latest improved farm machinery. One such man is worth as much to the general industrial interests of a country as three "farm hands." No country can be very prosperous unless the people who cultivate the soil own it and live on it. I repeat, then, that one of my first thoughts in beginning agricultural training at the Tuskegee Institute was to help to replace the "farm hand" of the South with something better.

As an illustration of the need of new ideas in farming, and of the effect that the long-continued cultivation of a single crop has upon the tiller, I remember that some years ago I invited a farmer into my office and explained to him in detail how he could make thirty dollars an acre on his land if he would plant a portion of it in sweet potatoes, whereas if he planted cotton, as he had been doing for years, he could make only fifteen dollars per acre in the best season. As I explained the difference, step by step, he agreed with me at every point, and when I came near to the end of my argument I began to congratulate myself that I had converted at least one man from the one-crop system to better methods. Finally, with what I fear was the air of one who felt that he had won his case, I asked the farmer what he was going to cultivate on his land the coming year. The old fellow scratched his head, and said that as he was getting old, and had been growing cotton all his life, he reckoned he would grow it to the end of his few remaining years, although he agreed with me that he could double the product of his land by planting sweet potatoes on it.

Soon after we had succeeded in clearing the trees and stumps from a few acres of ground, we planted a small crop. This crop, as I have stated, was not very different from others which the students had seen planted or had taken part in planting at their homes, because the school was poor in implements and stock. The main difference between our first crop and those which the students had come into contact with at their homes was that ours was to some extent a diversified crop. The increasing number of students soon made it necessary to increase the acreage of land cultivated. In the first few months of the Tuskegee Institute the students boarded in families. This made it difficult to get the greatest value out of our farm products. Partly to overcome this, we arranged to begin boarding the students upon the school grounds. Here another difficulty presented itself. It was found that a student would be of little value to the farm and would gain very little in knowledge and skill if he worked only a few hours each day. We discovered that, after there had been subtracted the minutes required for him to reach his work, get his tools, and otherwise prepare himself, little time would be left for getting actual results out of the soil. In order to overcome this weakness in our system, we decided to follow in some measure the plan originated by General Armstrong at the Hampton Institute. This was to have the students study in the class rooms during four days of the week, and work on the farm two days. The students, however, for a long while referred to these two days as "lost days."

It was often amusing, as well as interesting, to note the intense faith of the students in their books. The larger the book and the bigger the words it contained, the more highly it was revered. At this time there were almost no text-books which dealt with industrial subjects. For this reason, any one who wanted to give instructions in such branches had, in a very large measure, to "blaze" his way. The absence of text-books on these subjects made it all the more difficult at first to combine industrial and academic teaching. We partly solved the problem by having the students work two days at some industry and study four days in the school-room.

We found it advisable to consider not only the best system of teaching in our practical work, but the economic values also. We felt that it would be possible to teach the students the latest and best methods of performing all kinds of hand work, and at the same time show them the dignity of such service. But in addition to this we wanted the students to do such work as they could about the school, work which otherwise would have been done by hired men not connected with the institution.

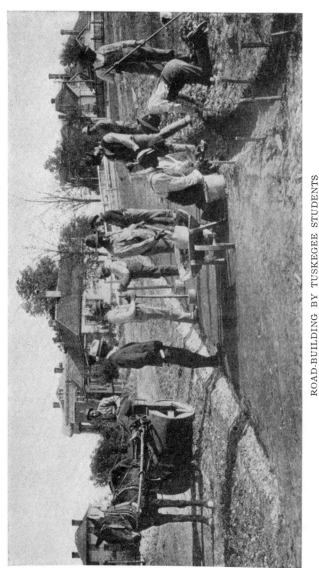

ROAD-BUILDING BY TUSKEGEE STUDENTS

We felt, therefore, that the fair thing to do would be to arrange some scheme by which the student would receive compensation for all the work of value which he did for the school. This we felt was not only just, but would emphasise another valuable element in teaching. The lack of this economic emphasis I have always felt to be one of the weak points in manual training. To enable us to meet this condition, we decided to have the students board on the school grounds, to charge them eight dollars per month for their board, and then to give them credit on their board-bills for all the work they did which proved to have productive or money-saving value.

Aside from the economic results of the work, we knew that the mere effort on the part of the student to help himself through school by labour would prevent our making "hot-house plants" of our students, and would prove worth while in character building. In all cases payment for work depended upon the individual efforts of the students. One of the dominating purposes kept always in mind was to give the student a chance to help himself by means of some industry. In this connection, I beg to say that in my judgment the whole problem of the future of my race hinges largely upon the question: "To what extent will the Negro, when given a chance, help himself, and make himself indispensable to the community in which he lives?"

We soon learned that in the practical application of our scheme the average student would earn from two to three dollars a month by working two days in the week, leaving only five or six dollars to be paid in cash. Some students were so much in earnest that they worked out more than half of the eight dollars. This opportunity proved a godsend to most of the students, as very few of them were able to pay the eight dollars a month in cash during nine months of the year. Aside from other considerations, we began to find out that we could quickly test the worth of a student by the degree of earnestness which he evinced in helping himself through labour with his hands. After a little while, many of the students began to take great pride in telling their parents at the end of each month how much they had helped themselves through their work on the farm or in other industries. This information and enthusiasm came in time to have its influence in leading the parents to appreciate the value of hand training.

As the school grew in size and experience, it became apparent that we ought to find a way to help the large number of young men and women who were constantly seeking admission, but who had no money with which to pay any portion of their expenses. We became convinced that some of the most promising and worthy students were those who came from the country districts, where

they had had very few advantages of book
education. They had little or no money, but
they had good strong bodies, and were not ashamed
to work with their hands. In reaching this class of
students I found that my experience at the Hampton
Institute was of great advantage. We decided to
start a night school for students who could not
afford to go to school in the day time. The number who availed themselves of this arrangement was
very small at first. We began by making a written
contract with each student to the effect that he or
she was to work during the whole of the day at
some industry, and study in the class room for two
hours at night, after the day's work was completed.
In order to put this plan upon a sound basis, the
following form of contract was signed:

TUSKEGEE NORMAL AND INDUSTRIAL INSTITUTE.

(INCORPORATED.)

This agreement, made the seventeenth day of October, 1902,
between James C. Black, of the first part, and Booker T. Washington, Principal of The Tuskegee Normal and Industrial
Institute, of the second part,

Witnesseth, that the said James C. Black has agreed faithfully, carefully and truly to serve The Tuskegee Normal and
Industrial Institute, in whatever capacity the said Booker T.
Washington, Principal, etc., or those deputed by him, may
designate, from date hereof to the seventeenth day of October,
1904.

In consideration of service to be rendered by James C. Black, the said Booker T. Washington, Principal, etc., has agreed to allow said James C. Black eight dollars per month, provided he remains until October 17, 1904; otherwise he has agreed to pay him at the rate of one-fifth of that sum per month for the time he may have been in the service of The Tuskegee Normal and Industrial Institute; this latter amount to include all amounts which may have been charged against said James C. Black.

It is agreed, further, that the amount earned shall be reserved in the hands of the said Booker T. Washington, Principal, etc., the same to be used in paying the expenses of said James C. Black in the regular classes of The Tuskegee Normal and Industrial Institute. In case the said James C. Black leaves school voluntarily, or is dismissed after the expiration of the time for which he agrees to serve, he is to forfeit all that the school may owe him at that time.

It is further agreed that no part of what said James C. Black may earn shall be transferred to another's account, but shall be kept for James C. Black's exclusive use after he shall have entered the Day School.

It is distinctly understood that what said James C. Black may earn is for the purpose of paying board, and no part can be drawn in cash.

In witness whereof, we have hereunto set our hands and seals.

JAMES C. BLACK (L. S.)
BOOKER T. WASHINGTON (L. S.)

WITNESS: { ABRAM T. BLACKETT
          { GEORGE F. MAY

CHAPTER V

BUILDING UP A SYSTEM

THE system we decided to use at Tuskegee divided the school into two classes of students: those who worked with their hands two days in the week, and spent four days in the class room; and the night students, who, through the first year of their course, worked all day with their hands and spent their evenings in the class rooms. Of course, the student who worked ten hours each day was paid more than the one who laboured only two days in the week. The night-school students were to earn, not only their board, but something in addition. The surplus was to be used in paying their expenses in the regular day school after they had remained in the night school one or two years as they might elect. The night school, besides other opportunities, gave the student a chance to get a start in his books and also in some trade or industry. With this as a foundation, I have rarely seen a student who was worth much fail to pass through the regular course.

The night school had not been in session many weeks before several facts began to make themselves prominent. The first was the economic value of the work of the night students. It was plain that these students could perform much labour for which we should otherwise have had to pay out cash to persons not connected with the institution. It is true that the work at first was crude, but it should be remembered that in the earlier years the whole school was crude. All work in laying the foundation for a race is crude.

The economic value of hand work at the Tuskegee Institute can be illustrated in no better way than by data of the construction of our buildings. When a friend has given us twenty-five thousand dollars for a building, instead of having it constructed by an outside contractor, we have had the students produce the material and do the work as far as possible, and through this method a large proportion of the money given for the building passes into the hands of the students, to be used in gaining an education. The plan has a double value, for, in addition to the twenty-five thousand dollars which is diverted into channels through which a large number of students get an education, the school receives the building for permanent use.

Let us value the work at Tuskegee by this test: The plans for the Slater-Armstrong Memorial Trades' Building, in its main dimensions 283 x 315 feet, and two stories high, were drawn by a coloured man, our instructor in mechanical drawing. Eight hundred

BUILDING A NEW DORMITORY

Students draw plans, dig foundations, make the brick, cut timber, which they saw and make into joists and frames. The painting, plastering, plumbing and roofing are also done by the students under the direction of their instructors

thousand bricks were required in its construction, and every one of them was manufactured by our students while learning the trade of brick-making. All the bricks were laid into the building by students who were being taught the trade of brickmasonry. The plastering, carpentry work, painting, and tin-roofing were done by students while learning these trades. The whole number of students who received training on this building alone was 196. It is lighted by electricity, and all the electric fixtures were put in by students who were learning electrical engineering. The power to operate the machinery in this building comes from a 125 horse-power engine and a 75 horse-power boiler. All this machinery was not only operated by students who were learning the trade of steam engineering, but was installed by students under the guidance of their instructor.

For other examples of the amount of work that our students do in the direction of self-help, I would mention the fact that they manufactured 2,990,000 bricks during the past twelve months; 1,367 garments of various kinds have been made in the tailor shop, and 541,837 pieces have been laundered in the laundry division by the girls.

Agriculture is the industry which we plan to make stand out most prominently; and we expect more and more to base much of our other training upon this fundamental industry. There are two reasons why we have not been able to send out as many students from our agricultural department as we have desired:

First, agriculture was the industry most disliked by the students and their parents in the earlier years of the school. It required nearly ten years to overcome this prejudice.

Second, nearly all of our buildings, seventy-two in number, have been built by the students, and the building trades have, of necessity, been emphasised. As soon as the building period slackens, we shall be able to send out a larger number skilled in all the branches of agriculture.

I have been asked many times about the progress of the students in the night school as compared with those in the day school. In reality, there is little difference. A student who studies two hours at night and works with his hands ten hours during the day, naturally covers less ground in the text-books than the day student, yet in real sound growth and the making of manhood, I question whether the day student has much advantage over the student in the night school. There is an indescribable something about work with the hands that tends to develop a student's mind. The night-school students take up their studies with a degree of enthusiasm and alertness that is not equalled in the day classes. I have known instances where a student seemed so dull or stupid that he made practically no progress in the study of books. He was away

DIGGING FOUNDATION FOR A NEW BUILDING ON THE INSTITUTE GROUNDS

from the books entirely for a few months and put to work at a trade; at the end of a few months he has returned to the class room, and it has been surprising to note how much more easily he could master the text-books than before. There is something, I think, in the handling of a tool that has the same relation to close, accurate thinking that writing with a pen has in the preparation of a manuscript. Nearly all persons who write much will agree, I think, that one can produce much more satisfactory work by using the pen than by dictation.

While speaking of the effect of careful hand training on the development of character, it is worth while to mention an uncommonly instructive example. If any one goes into a community North or South, and asks to have pointed out to him the man of the Negro race of the old generation, who stands for the best things in the life of the coloured community, in six cases out of ten, I venture to say, he will be shown a man who learned a trade during the days of slavery. A few years ago, James Hale, a Negro, died in Montgomery, Alabama. He spent the greater part of his life as a slave. He left property valued at fifty thousand dollars, and bequeathed a generous sum to be used in providing for an infirmary for the benefit of his race. James Hale could not read or write a line, yet I do not believe that there is a white or black man in Montgomery who knew Mr. Hale who will not agree with me in saying that he was the first coloured citizen of Montgomery. I have seldom met a man of any race who surpassed him in sterling qualities. When Mr. Hale was a slave his master took great pains to have him well trained as a carpenter, contractor and builder. His master saw that the better the slave was trained in handicraft, the more dollars he was worth. In my opinion, it was this hand-training, despite the evil of slavery, that largely resulted in Mr. Hale's fine development. If Mr. Hale was all this with mere hand training, what might he have been if his mind had also been carefully educated? Mr. Hale was simply a type of many men to be found in nearly every part of the country.

The average manual-training school has for its main object the imparting of culture to the student; while the economic element is made secondary. At the Tuskegee Institute we have always emphasised the trade or economic side of education. With any ignorant and poverty-stricken race, I believe that the problem of bread-winning should precede that of culture. For this reason the students who have attended the night school at Tuskegee have, as a rule, mastered the principles and practice of agriculture, or have been taught a trade by means of which we felt sure they could earn a living. With the question of shelter, food and clothing settled, there is a basis for what are considered the higher and more important things.

We have, therefore, emphasised the earning value of education rather than the finished manual training, being careful at the same time to lay the foundations of thorough moral, mental and religious instruction. In following this method something may be lost of the accuracy and finish which could be obtained if a course in manual training preceded the industrial course, but the fact that the student is taught the principles of house-building in building a real house, and not a play house, gives him a self-reliance and confidence in his ability to make a living, that manual training alone could not give. The boy in the conditions surrounding the average Negro youth, leaving school with manual training alone, finds himself little better off than he was before, so far as his immediate and pressing problem of earning a living is concerned. He and those dependent upon him want at once food, shelter, clothing and the opportunity to live properly in a home. Industrial education takes into consideration the economic element in production in a way that manual training does not, and this is of great value to a race just beginning its career.

While I am speaking of the comparative value of manual training and industrial education, there is one other difference between them to which I ought to call attention. The proportion of students who complete an industrial or trade course is likely to be smaller than the proportion completing a literary or manual training course.   For example, a boy comes to Tuskegee Institute, as has often happened, from a district where he has been earning fifty cents a day.   At Tuskegee he works at the brickmason's trade for nine months.   He cannot master the trade during this time, but he gets a start in it.   At the end of the nine-months' session, if he returns home, this student finds himself in demand in the community, at wages which range from one dollar and a half to two dollars a day.   Unless he is a man of extraordinarily strong character, he will be likely to yield to the temptation to remain at home, and become a rather commonplace mason, instead of returning and finishing his trade, in order that he may become a master workman.   So far I have been unable to discover any remedy that will completely offset this tendency.   The most effective cure for it, so far as my experience is concerned, is an appeal to the pride of the student.

Another question often asked me is, how long it will take an industrial school to become self-supporting.   To this question I always reply that I know of no industrial school that is self-supporting, nor do I believe that any school which performs its highest functions as an industrial school will become so.   I believe that it is the duty of all such schools to make the most of the economic element—to make

AT WORK IN THE SCHOOL'S BRICK-YARD
Getting a kiln ready to fire

each industry pay in dollars and cents just as far as is possible—but the element of teaching should be made the first consideration, and the element of production secondary. Very often at the Tuskegee Institute it would pay the institution better to keep a boy away from the farm than to have him spend a day at work on it; but the farm is for the boy, and not the boy for the farm.

An industrial school is continually at work on raw material. When a student gets to the point where he can build a first-class wagon or buggy, he is not retained at the school to build these vehicles merely for their economic value, but is sent out into the world to begin his life's work; and another student is taken in his place to begin the work afresh. The cost of teaching the new student and the waste of material weigh heavily against the cost of production. Hence, it can easily be seen that it is an almost impossible task to make money out of an industrial school, or to make it self-supporting. The moment the idea of " making it pay " is placed uppermost, the institution becomes a factory, and not a school for training head and hand and heart.

One of the advantages of the night school at Tuskegee is in the sifting-out process of the student body. Unless a student has real grit in him and means business, he will not continue very long to work with his hands ten hours a day for the privilege of studying two hours at night. Though much of the work done by students at an industrial school like Tuskegee does not pay, the mere effort at self-help on the part of the student is of the greatest value in character building.

Most races have come up through contact with the soil, either directly or indirectly.   There is something about the smell of the soil—a contact with a reality that gives one a strength and development that can be gained in no other way.   In advocating industrial training for backward or weak races or individuals, I have always kept in mind the strengthening influence of contact with a real thing, rather than with a third-rate imitation of a thing.

The great lesson which the race needs to learn in freedom is to work willingly, cheerfully and efficiently. In laying special stress upon hand training for a large proportion of my race, I ask no peculiar education for the Negro, because he is a Negro, but I would advocate the same training for the German, the Jew, or the Frenchman, were he in the same relative stage of racial development as the masses of the Negroes.   While insisting upon thorough and high-grade industrial education for a large proportion of my race, I have always had the greatest sympathy with first-class college training and have recognised the fact that the Negro race, like other races, must have thoroughly trained college men and women. There is a place and a work for such, just as there is a place and a work for those thoroughly trained with their hands.

I shall never forget a remark I once heard made by a lady of foreign birth. She had recently arrived in America, and by chance had landed in one of our largest American cities. As she was a woman of considerable importance, she received lavish social attention. For weeks her life was spent in a round of fashionable dressing, dining, automobiling, balls, theaters, art museums, card parties, and what not. When she was quite worn out, a friend took her to visit the Hampton Normal and Agricultural Institute. There she saw students and teachers at work in the soil, in wood, in metal, in leather, at work cooking, sewing, laundering. She saw a company of the most devoted men and women in the world giving their lives in the most unselfish manner, that they might help to put a race on its feet. It was then that she exclaimed in my presence: "What a relief! Here I have found a reality; and I am so glad that I did not leave America before I saw it."

I think I was able to understand something of her feeling. In the history of the Negro race since freedom, one of the most difficult tasks has been to teach the teachers and leaders to exercise enough patience and foresight to keep the race down to a reality, instead of yielding to the temptations to grasp after shadows and superficialities.   But the race itself is learning the lesson very fast.   Indeed, the rank and file learn faster than some of the teachers and leaders.

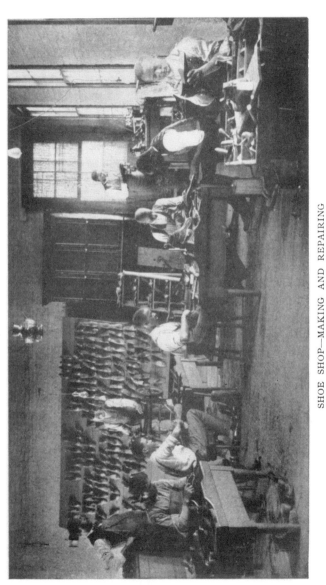

SHOE SHOP—MAKING AND REPAIRING

CHAPTER VI

WELDING THEORY AND PRACTICE

BROOM-MAKING has been recently included among the industries for girls at Tuskegee. Hundreds of brooms were being worn out every year in sweeping the floors of more than seventy buildings; and I venture to say that more brooms were used up for the same amount of floor space than at almost any other institution of the kind. Wherever you may go in the shops, or halls, you will find some one busy with a broom most of the time. The litter in the carpenter shop or the mattress-making room is not allowed to accumulate until the end of the day, but is swept up so often that visitors sometimes ask me whether there is a moment of the working day when some one is not wielding a busy broom somewhere in the institution.

It was this reason that inspired the home manufacture of the needed supply of brooms. It had been found possible to supply most of the needs of the school by student labour, and after establishing a summer canning factory, which Chaplain Penney directs while the Bible School is not in session, making brooms seemed a natural evolution of

supply and demand.   But investigation showed
that none of the instructors knew anything about
making brooms, and that the Experimental Farm
had not yet taken up the task of raising broom-
corn.   These obstacles were not serious in comparison with many others which had been attacked
in the industrial school.

A way was found to make the first sample
broom, and gradually the needed machinery
was installed.   Then the director of the Agricultural Department discovered that broom-corn
could be raised on the farm, and now students
can be equipped to take the industrial knowledge
home with them, and also to grow the crop
on their own farms.   This department keeps
the school supplied with good brooms at small
cost, and out of a minor need grew another
useful industry.   The lesson in this little story
is that finding a way to solve the problems
closest at home helps to build up the community at large.   It was found, also, that the
work of the class room could be correlated even
with broom-making, and made to harmonise
with the Tuskegee theory of education of head
and hands together.   The girls were asked to
write compositions descriptive of their work in
this industry, and some of these efforts have been
very creditable.

I insert one of these compositions as a sample:

MATTRESS-MAKING

All the mattresses and pillows used at the Institute are made by the students

"BROOM-MAKING"

"I am a nice large broom just made Tuesday by Harriet McCray. Before I was made into a broom, I grew over in a large farm with a great many others of my sisters. One day I was cut down and brought up to the broom-making department, and was carefully picked to pieces to get the best straw. I was put in a machine called the winder. Here I was wound very tightly, and then put in another machine called the press. I was pressed out flat and sewed tightly. Out of the press I was carried to the clipper, and all of my seed and long ends were cut off. From the cutter I was carried to the threshing machine and combed out thoroughly, and put in the barrel for sale. I was sold to the school for thirty-five cents. He will use me very roughly in doors, and when I begin to get old, I shall be used in sweeping the yards. When I am worn completely out, I shall be pulled to pieces to get my handle, which will be used again to make a fresh, new broom."

Class-room work is also made a part of the training in this varied catalogue of industries in successful operation at Tuskegee: Agriculture, basketry, blacksmithing, bee-keeping, brick-masonry, plastering, brick-making, carpentry, carriage trimming, cooking, dairying, architectural, free-hand and mechanical drawing, plain sewing, dress-making, electrical and steam engineering, founding, harness-making, house-keeping, horticulture, canning, laundering, machinery, mattress making, millinery, nurses' training, painting, saw-milling, shoe-making, printing, stock-raising, tailoring, tinning, and wheel-wrighting.

It will be seen that the school is a community unto itself, in which buildings can be erected, finished, and furnished, the table supplied the year round, and economic independence achieved in a large measure. But this work is for the benefit of the student, not to make the school self-supporting. Therefore, no one side of his education must be neglected in order that he may be for the time a more productive labourer in his department of industry. It would be wronging both him and the system to keep him at the work-bench all the working hours in order that he might turn out the greatest possible number of shoes, or window sashes, or fruit cans in a week.

For example, if you should chance to visit the carpenter shop, you would find a score of young men turning out the finished material for some new building in process of erection, or at the lathes turning out the interior finishings. But in a small room in one corner, having a hard time to be heard above the din of the steam saws, is an instructor with a class of students, who are learning to draw up contracts for jobs in carpentry or building.

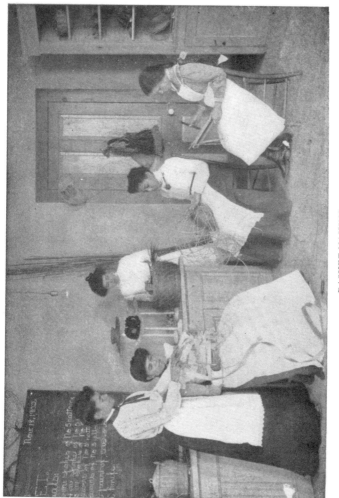

BASKET-MAKING

Special effort is made to have the students use the natural products of the region as material

They are not going out with the expectation of always being carpenters at day wages. They should know how to make contracts as "boss carpenters," to build houses, or repair them, or how to hire other men to build houses for them. Therefore, they learn to draw up specifications in both legal and practical form, so that when the occasion arises they will know how to work with intelligence.

Their class-room work in spelling, mathematics, grammar, and English composition comes effectively into play. They find out that a carpenter has small chance of getting ahead unless he can use his head intelligently. He writes out a contract, for example, to put up a four-room house, on a basis of three cash payments—when he takes the job; when the roof is on; and when the house is turned over to the owner. This contract is read aloud by the instructor, who asks the other members of the class to criticise it. One of them points out a flaw which would allow the owner to "crawl out" of his bargain on a technicality. Another is pleased to discover that the arithmetic is so faulty that the estimates of the cost of material would land the contractor in the poor-house. Then the student begins to see that his so-called academic teaching is as important in his calling as his skill with the plane, the saw and the miter-box, and that he cannot hope to become a good carpenter unless he is also a diligent scholar.

In the winter an instructor in the Agricultural Classes may teach his students to familiarise themselves, through books, with insect pests which infest the peach tree. They are asked to give their own ideas of the "borer," or the "scale," but this information is not allowed to be packed away in the attic of memory, to be forgotten like so much useless lumber. The real examination comes in the spring, not in written papers, but in the school orchard. The same instructor takes the class among the peach trees, and, with branches in their hands, they are required to identify the "borer," and apply to the trees the remedies laid down in their books and lectures.

When a new building is to be erected, the school industries join their activities in a common cause. The project sets in motion, first, the wagons to be used in removing the excavated material. The young men in the wheelwright, blacksmithing, and harness-making rooms see their work tested, for they have made and equipped all the heavy farm wagons needed for this hauling. Along with their daily work with the hands, the patterns and instructions had been given them on blackboards and in lectures. They have trained their minds, they have learned handicraft, and the combined results are applied. Their wagons and harness are not

IN THE SCHOOL'S SAWMILL

to be sent away or put on exhibition. They must stand the strain at home, and if they are faulty it cannot be hidden.

Then come the brick-makers, turning out 20,000 bricks a day in the school kilns. They know whether they have made good bricks when they see them handled, and put into the walls by the student masons. In the course for brick-masonry, there is practical demonstration the year round. All the brick work on the buildings of the school is done by students, under the supervision of the instructors. Plastering and repair work, both inside and outside of the buildings, is in charge of the Brickmasonry Division. The theory is taught in the class room, the practical test is always close at hand. The brick-mason and plasterer has one hundred and eighteen lessons in the fundamental principles of the trade, he is taught how to make estimates on different kinds of work, he has a course in architectural drawing, and he does research work in trade journals. So much for theory, but his diploma of efficient mastery of his trade is built into the walls of the Tuskegee buildings. They show whether he has learned to be a brick-mason, or whether he has merely learned things about brick-masonry.

The school sawmill turns out the lumber for the building in course of erection. The instruction in saw-milling includes these branches of information:

"Names of machines and their uses. Care of machines. Defects of timber trees. Felling timber trees and loading logs on wagon. Measuring lumber and wood. Industrial classes. Drawing. Scaling logs to find their contents in board measure. Grading lumber. Running planer and other machines. Care of belts. Saw filing and caring for saws. Designing and making cutters for mouldings. Calculating speed of pulleys. Arrangment of machines in a planing and saw mill, etc."

Theory and practice in this department are dovetailed in the finished work in the interior of such a structure as the Carnegie Library, or the new Collis P. Huntington Memorial Building, where the wood work, handsomely finished in Southern pine, is the product of the school saw-mill and planer, the carpenter shops and the paint-shop.

The equipment of the machinery, engineering, and foundry department and the courses of study offered are designed to give students a thorough training in their various branches. The machine shop is equipped with the latest machine tools, driven by power from an Atlas engine. All the repair work on the mechanical equipment of the school, including steam pumps, steam engines, woodworking machines, printing presses, metal working machines, is done in this shop. About fifty different machines outside of this department, including the complete steam laundry, the agricultural and

IN THE MACHINE-SHOP

Three years are required to complete this course

dairy machinery, are in daily operation, furnishing the best possible demonstration of the theory taught in the classes. In the course for steam engineers, the young men are able to study the working of eleven different steam engines, seven steam pumps, twelve steam boilers, and a complete water-works system, with miles of piping, valves, gauges, recording apparatus, etc. The instructors lay out the courses in theory and written work, and the mathematical studies are applied in work on blue-print drawings and free-hand sketches.

A foundry is in daily operation, and here the castings used in repair work for the school are made. When the Tuskegee cotton-raising party went to Africa, the castings for the cotton press sent with them were made in the school foundry. In the plumbing and steam-fitting division, the tools and shop equipment are ample for training in lead and iron work, for water and steam piping systems in buildings of various kinds. The plumbing and steam fitting in nearly all the buildings of the Institute were done by the classes of this division. This work includes sinks, bath-tubs, steam radiators, lavatories and sanitary closets. More than eight miles of piping of various sizes, for steam and water, are in use on the school grounds, with all the necessary valves, expansion joints, unions and fittings. The tinsmithing shop turns out nearly every kind of tin work from covering a house to making a pepper-box. The apprentice becomes a first-class tinsmith in two years' training. More than two thousand one-gallon fruit cans were made by the students last year in addition to many other useful articles.

The object of the course in electrical engineering is to give the student a foundation upon which he may build along any special line he may choose later. Arc and incandescent lighting is in use at the school, and there is a complete telephone service connecting most of the buildings and offices through a central station. The students learn not only how to install these systems, but to maintain them in the highest state of efficiency. The dynamos and other electrical machinery of a complete power-house are in operation for lighting the school buildings and grounds, so that the student finds practical work at every turn in his course.

He has learned how to build and equip a building. He is taught also how to design it in all its parts. All students in the day and night schools who are in the Mechanical Department are required to take instruction in mechanical drawing. The work of the first year is largely preparatory. It begins with simple geometrical drawing, to accustom the student to the use of instruments and to teach him accuracy and neatness. This is followed by work in projection, which finds application in scale-drawing of simple objects. As soon as a fair

STUDENTS AT WORK IN THE SCHOOL'S FOUNDRY

knowledge of the instruments has been attained, with a thorough drill in free-hand sketching, the study of design is carried far enough to secure an understanding of the principles, and facility and accuracy in the construction of drawing plans. Strictly speaking, mechanical drawing begins with the second year of trade work, with the study of materials and working drawings. During the last quarter of the third year the student learns how to make blue, solar, and black prints. During the fourth year several excursions are made by the class to the shops, the buildings under construction, the brick-yard, etc. In such excursions detailed notes must be taken and a satisfactory report submitted upon the things seen and examined.

The course of architectural drawing covers three years, and aims to give thorough instruction in drawing, building construction and design. In all cases, the general mechanical and artistic training is supplemented by the course of study in the Academic Department. On entering the third year of the architectural course, the student, in addition to his regular work, is given actual practice in office training and general superintendence. The student visits also the trade shops, and is required to attend classes in heating, electrical lighting, and plumbing. Many of the most satisfactory and imposing buildings of the school were designed in our architectural department.

It will be seen from the foregoing survey that the students are able to build and equip a large building from top to bottom, inside and out, and these object lessons of their own handiwork stand clustered over many acres, a city in itself built by young coloured men, most of whom were wholly ignorant of systematic mental or manual training when they asked to be admitted to Tuskegee.

They maintain also what may be called the running machinery of the institution. The carpenters learn wood-turning and cabinet-making. They make the furniture used in the class rooms and dormitories. Their regular division has been so crowded in recent years that it was found necessary to organise an auxiliary division, called the "Repair Shop." Here all the school's repairs in wood work are done, and the training has proved so valuable that it has been made a separate course of study extending over three years. In the blacksmith shop is performed the ironing of carriages, buggies, and wagons, of which a hundred are used by the school, in addition to making all kinds of implements and the shoeing of horses. Hundreds of farm implements are repaired here. The student blacksmith is not a mere labourer. He is taught how to run a shop of his own. He learns how to make out bills for material, how to keep shop supplies, and a part of his time is devoted to mechanical drawing and class room work.

CLASS IN MECHANICAL DRAWING

The division of wheelwrighting is fitted for work in all details of the trade. The students have constantly on hand new work, such as the building of wagons, drays, horse and hand carts, wheel-barrows, buggies and road carts. A great deal of repair work must be done to keep the farm equipment in first-class shape, and the shop is constantly patronised for this kind of work by the farmers of the town and neighbourhood. The school has a standing order for farm wagons from merchants in Tuskegee and Montgomery. These are turned out complete, and have proved serviceable and popular. All of the harness used by the school, and a large quantity sold outside, is made in the harness-making department. All the vehicles turned out by the blacksmith and wheelwrighting divisions are finished by the students in the carriage-trimming shop.

The visitor, therefore, who wishes to inspect the Tuskegee Institute, is met at the station by a carriage built by the students, pulled by horses raised on the school farms, whose harness was made in a school shop. The driver wears a trim, blue uniform made in the school tailor-shop, and shoes made by student class work. The visitor is assigned to a guest room in a dormitory designed, built, and furnished by the students. His bathroom plumbing, the steam heat in his room, and the electric lighting were installed by students. The oak furniture of his room came from the shops. The young woman who takes care of his room is a student working her way through the Institute. After supper, she will change her wearing apparel to a blue uniform dress and a neat straw hat, all made in the school. The steam laundry sends over to know if the visitor wishes some washing done, and girl students send it back, proud of the snowy polish of shirts and collars. The visitor is asked to be a guest in the teachers' dining-hall. The bill of fare may read as follows:

BREAKFAST:

Breakfast food, ham, fried cakes, bread, syrup, coffee, tea, butter, fruit.

DINNER:

Roast beef, tomatoes, rice, corn-bread, sweet potatoes, buttermilk, snap beans, dessert.

SUPPER:

Cold ham, tea, bread, syrup, butter, milk, fried potatoes, coffee.

In looking over this program, the guest will discover that the ham, roast beef, vegetables, corn-bread, syrup, butter, milk, and potatoes are products of the school farms, raised, cared for and produced by student labour.

Throughout these varied fields of industrial and productive activity, the following objects are kept constantly in view, and their relative importance is in the order of their enumeration:

To teach the dignity of labour.

THE BLACKSMITH SHOP

To teach the trades, thoroughly and effectively.

To supply the demand for trained industrial leaders.

To assist the students in paying all, or a part, of their expenses.

CHAPTER VII

HEAD AND HANDS TOGETHER

THAT the distinctive feature of Tuskegee Institute—ample provision for industrial training—has received in the public prints almost exclusive attention is not strange. But it is well to remember that Tuskegee Institute stands for education as well as for training, for men and women as well as for bricks and mortar.

Of course, the distinction involved in the words, "education" and "training," is largely theoretical. My experience convinces me that training to some productive trade, be it wagon-building or farming, educates. For example, one of our students is foreman on the large and beautifully planned Collis P. Huntington Memorial Building, now in process of construction; that young man is notable for a simple honesty, an unobtrusive confidence and self-reliance, that abundantly testify to his manliness. That this manliness is in large degree directly traceable to his skill and his experience in bearing industrial responsibility—in short, to his training—is beyond peradventure. Indeed, in running over the long list of students who, for one reason or another

—lack of money or lack of taste for books—have left Tuskegee without completing the prescribed course in the Academic Department, I have been forcibly impressed with the fact that training to productive industry directly tends to develop sound judgment and manly independence—those qualities of the mind and heart that collectively constitute the character of the educated man.

Another example of the effect of the training given at the Tuskegee Institute on the mind of the student occurs to me. A few weeks ago it was decided to modify the Day School system. To make any change in a great organisation like ours requires great discriminating judgment and care. The faculty discussed the change in its every phase, and I finally called the students of the four upper classes together, presented to them our plans, and explained to them the reasons for the proposed change.

Their response was not a negative acquiescence, but a series of direct and searching questions. They were alert and quick to see minor defects, and to give direct and constructive criticism in regard to many details. Their work in the shops and on the farm had brought them into touch with real issues and real things—their daily work in constructing and equipping our buildings and in helping to build the institute had brought with it an intelligent interest in the school and an enlightened appreciation of values; in other words, it had taught them to think.

It is obvious that a man cannot build wagons or run a farm with continuous success who is unable to read, write, and cipher. But, far deeper than the mere commercial advantage of academic studies, is the fact that they afford incentives to good conduct and high thinking. To make a boy an efficient mechanic is good, for it enables him to earn a living and to add his mite to the productiveness of society; but a school must do more—must create in him abiding interests in the intellectual achievements of mankind in art and literature, and must stimulate his spiritual nature. And so Tuskegee has always maintained an Academic Department, at present housed mainly in four buildings. The most important of these are Porter Hall, a three-story frame building, the first building erected after the opening of the Institute, though poor in appointments, yet rich in traditions; Thrasher Hall, a handsome three-story brick building with well-equipped physical and chemical laboratories; and the Carnegie Library, a beautifully proportioned brick structure, which is the center of Academic interests. The collection of books is well selected, and the generosity of Tuskegee's friends keeps it constantly growing. The admirable Collis P. Huntington Memorial Building will be the largest building on the grounds, and is to be used exclusively for academic purposes.

On the faculty of the Academic Department are

STUDENTS FRAMING THE ROOF OF A LARGE BUILDING

twenty-eight men and women of Negro blood with degrees from Michigan, Nebraska, Oberlin, Amherst, Cornell, Columbia, and Harvard.   In order to display the character of work done in the Department, it may be well for me to explain the course of study in some special branches.

The aim of the work in English in the preparatory classes is to bring about familiarity with the mother tongue, and correctness and ease in its use.   From contact with good models of spoken or written discourse the pupil learns to appreciate and interpret thought well expressed.   From the careful attention given his own language, he learns to feel the correctness or incorrectness of an expression, without slavish reliance upon rules.   In other words, in these classes language is taught as an art; the necessary rules and definitions, when they occur, are treated as working principles, and abundant practice in applying them is given.   In the advanced years of the course, technical grammar is taught because at this stage the pupil has already become familiar with good usage, and has attained a certain facility in employing the mother tongue.   He should now be taught more thoroughly the fundamental principles governing the correct or incorrect use of an expression, while in the preparatory classes, oral exercises in narration, description and reproduction predominate. The pupil is encouraged to talk simply and naturally about something he has seen or heard or read.   He is taught to exercise care for unity, logical sequence of ideas, and smoothness of transition. To the narration and description of the lower grades, argumentation and exposition are added in the advanced work, these subjects being expanded to form the basis of a course in public speaking.

The pupil obtains material for themes and debates from his experience in shop and field and from literature technical to the subject. The themes are submitted for correction and in due course committed, and, after preliminary training, delivered at the monthly public rhetoricals of the class. Except for the written brief required of each disputant, debates are extemporaneous. In the preparation of a program like the following, considerable experience and research must necessarily be involved.

" A " MIDDLE RHETORICAL

EVENING PRAYER SERVICE

A Model Southern Farm

"It is this noble agriculture which feeds the human race and all the humbler orders of animated nature dependent on man."
—Speech by EDWARD EVERETT

* * *

OVERTURE   ORCHESTRA
1 Choosing and Preparing the Land............*Leon Harris*
2 The Crops ....*Terry Hart*
    Song, "Old Folks at Home"..........*A Middle Quartette*
3 Constructing the Farm House..............*Alonzo Fields*
4 Constructing the Chimneys and Fireplaces..Charles Weir
    Duet........................*Miss Young, Mr. Weaver*

5 Care of the Farm House
    (a) The Dining-room and Kitchen......*Miss Emma Smith*
    (b) Bedrooms and Parlour..........*Miss Pearl Rousseau*
    Music..................Waltz...........*Orchestra*
6 The Kitchen Garden...............*Cornelius Richardson*
7 The Poultry-yard and Contents......*Miss Stella Pinkston*
    Music........................*A Middle Brass Quartett*
8 A Model Storage Barn.................*Thomas Brittain*
9 The Farm Machinery...................*William Lewis*
    Music..................March...........*Orchestra*
10 The Dairy Herd.....................*Mr. Wesley McCoy*
11 A Model Dairy-barn.................*Wm. J. Williams*
    Music.................Polka...........*Orchestra*

Exercises like the foregoing not only assist the Industrial Department in its work with the pupil, but offer admirable Academic training in English and in practical elocution. Besides the discussion relative to industrial pursuits, the pupils consider questions important to them as future citizens and men of business. This phase of the English work trains the pupil to rigorous methods of reasoning, and to clearness and forcefulness in public discourse.

Literature in the preparatory classes is taught under the head of reading. The physical requisites to effective expression receive due attention, but great stress is laid upon reading as a means by which the mind is furnished with knowledge. Literature is taught by reading and language teachers, the former dealing with the subject-matter for literary values, the latter having an eye to construction. The course is of twofold importance; contact with finished style gives to the pupil a sense of what is most fitting and beautiful in expression, thus proving an invaluable aid to his own oral and written diction. The work of the Senior class in English literature and composition aims to develop in the pupil power to think clearly and logically, and ability to appreciate thought expressed by others; to teach clearness and correctness of expression together with facility and power in the use of language; to produce an appreciation of good books by contact with classic authors; and to give, by an outline study of the history of English literature, a proper setting for the authors read. To supplement the class-room work in literature, a course in home reading has been arranged. It is the aim of the division of English to make the home reading as much like play as possible, a relaxation from sterner requirements of the curriculum, an occupation for idle hours. By persuading the most stupid pupil to read books which appeal to him, the teacher can lead him gradually to more solid literature.

As personal achievements appeal to the undeveloped mind more strongly than the chronicles of conflicts and political changes, the first course in history deals with biography. The student is given facts in the lives of men, Washington, Jefferson, Adams, and is made to feel that these men actually lived, that they are not mere abstract influences. At the very beginning their lives are

studied in the light of character building. After
the first ideas of character building have been
presented, the next step is to awaken the power of
the observation, to quicken the imagination. The
elementary course in English history is adapted to
this purpose.

The course in advanced American History is
for developing judgment and discrimination. Little
attention is given to the periods of discovery and
of colonisation, except to show the student how
the American people, as is true of all great nations,
began as cultivators of the soil.

The peculiar position of the Negro in American
History, from the earliest days of the slave trade,
through the wars with England and the Civil War,
to the present time, is given due importance, not
by isolating it, but by introducing it in its proper
place with other events.

In the Senior year, a course is given in the State
History of Alabama, for the benefit of those who
wish to fit themselves as teachers in that State.
The object is to acquaint the Normal student with
the important facts in the settlement of Alabama,
its entrance into the Union, and its present industrial
and political status.

During the first three years, the course in Geography is taught with Nature Study. In the last
year, Geography is combined with History. The
purpose of this arrangement is obvious. Geography

is really a broad phase of Nature Study. Questions regarding natural features, the sun, moon, planets, water-courses, physical points, etc., are explained in the course in Nature Study. Hence the pupil appreciates all the more what is said about them when he comes to them again in his Geography. The same intimacy is found in the study of plant and animal life, minerals, and rock formation.

Tuskegee is admirably fitted for the study of Geography, and every effort is made to make the teaching easily grasped. The industrial shops are always open to academic teachers and students. When the student takes up the subject of lumber, for example, he is able, by going to the shops, to understand the various stages through which the rough, uncut log must pass in order to make suitable building material. Then, too, the school grounds are put to excellent use. Various kinds of plant-life are studied; hills, valleys, small water-courses, examples of erosion, different kinds of soil, are seen on every hand. In connection with Nature Study and Geography, the pupils are urged to be on the alert to detect something new, something which they have seen often, but can afterward view in a new light because of the information obtained.

The course in mathematics covers a period of seven years, including Arithmetic, Algebra, Geometry, Trigonometry, and Surveying. Throughout the entire course, the aim is to give the student, as far

WOOD-TURNING MACHINERY.

as possible, a practical knowledge of the subjects embraced. The pupil is required to deal in things associated with figures, rather than with figures alone. In multiples and measures, his work is brought in close and effective touch with the trade work. For example, the carpenter must get the greatest common length of board from several different lengths without any waste: the dressmaker must find and use the smallest number of yards of cloth that suffice for the making of dresses of different sizes. Mathematics is shown to be an instrument of economy. In fractions, estimates are made of the cost of bales of cotton at prevailing prices. The student is often required to weigh out in each case the amounts of various articles which can be purchased for given amounts of money. In compound quantities and in the various measurements, the student does the measuring. Yards, rods, tons of coal, and tons of hay are measured. In carpeting, he is required to carpet a room. In lathing and plastering, he must witness the work in active operation. In percentage, problems which must be solved in the daily work the student is able to get from the industrial departments. For example, if the leather for a pair of shoes costs a definite amount, and the shoes are sold at a definite rate, what per cent. is gained? Or for what must they be sold so as to gain a certain per cent.?

Much actual outdoor work is done during the

study of trigonometry, and in surveying the student learns to lay off lots, country roads; to plot, map, etc. The last term of the Senior year is spent in mastering the elements of Civil Engineering, work for which the first two terms have prepared the student. The South is sorely in need of surveyors and men grounded in the elements of engineering; positions of this character are easy to find, and pay well.

The object of the work in Nature Study, as taught in the Academic Department, is to train the faculty of observation, create an interest in and love of nature, gain knowledge which will be of service in the future, and to cultivate a practical interest in Agriculture. Knowledge of things near at hand should be acquired first, and later of things more distant; a clear and definite acquaintance with home surroundings (plants, animals, minerals, natural phenomena, and the human body) is made the basis of the teaching as a foundation for more advanced study. In the assignment of work and selection of material for study, the special needs of special classes are kept in mind, the work being determined by the student's power of observation and interpretation. Subjects for study are selected largely according to the seasons. This work is conducted with reference to its correlation with Geography, language, and other subjects. Field excursions, collecting and preserving specimens, and gardening of various kinds, are prominent features of the courses in Nature Study.

The school offers also through the Academic Department, a two-years' course, especially treating of the affairs of the farm. Instruction is by laboratory work, supplemented by text-books, lectures, and reference readings, which are assigned from standard volumes and periodicals. The student is brought into close practical contact with his subject. He studies farm implements, traces root systems of corn and other crops, tests germination of seeds, determines the properties of soils and the effects of various crops and of rotation of crops upon soil fertility. He tests milk, studies butter and cheese, and judges a variety of animals.

The school owns an ample supply of plows, cultivators, planters, cutters, engines, etc. It has extensive collections of agricultural plants, seeds and products. Laboratories are well equipped with apparatus for the study of manures, fertilisers, soil bacteriology, germination of seeds, and judging cotton and corn. The Institute grounds and the fields and orchards of the Experiment Station are always available for illustrations in class work. Collections of seeds and woods, cabinets of beneficial and noxious insects, photographs, maps, charts, and drawings afford valuable material for study and demonstration. Specimens of draft and coach horses, Jersey, Ayrshire and Holstein cattle, Southdown sheep, and Berkshire swine, afford material for judging. In the Dairy Division is a complete outfit for cream separation and butter and cheese making. We have, also, levels, microscopes, and an extensive list of agricultural journals, a complete file of experiment station bulletins from all the States, and an excellent assortment of standard reference books.

The one purpose is to acquaint the student with the facts and principles needed for the improvement of soils, the increase of fertility, the nature of the various crops, the conditions governing their successful and economic production, and with the general development of agriculture. The student is also made familiar with animals, first, as to fitness for specific purposes; second, as to their care and management; third, as to their improvement by breeding; and fourth, as to the manufacture of animal products. He learns the principles of orchard management, small fruit culture, vegetable gardening and plant propagation, as well as the evolution of cultivated plants. A sense of the beautiful is cultivated and given expression in floriculture, to the end that more of nature's beauty shall pervade the home and its surroundings.

The work of each year of strictly mental education is prescribed. We aim to arouse the students' interest in important educational problems, with especial reference to the South, rewarding that interest with practical suggestions; and to train efficiently teachers who will render valuable service in school and society. The courses in Normal Education comprise a critical study of human nature; an outline history of American education; general and special methods in teaching; and school organisation and administration. The students in these courses observe expert teaching in a primary school under the direction of the Academic Department. Senior students are not only permitted to observe, but also to practice teaching under supervision. This division of Education is being strengthened, and keeps steadily before it the fact that Tuskegee is to send out teachers as well as trained artisans and industrial leaders.

The courses in Chemistry and in Physics, more clearly than any other Academic courses, complement the work of the Industrial Department. Thus in the course in Chemistry, operations in the shops and on the farm, involving chemical reactions, are drawn upon as illustrative material for the first year's work. The artisan, with a knowledge of chemical matters, grows and thinks, and is not automatic. The courses are not those in which the students are merely taught *how* to do, but *to do*. Soap is taken apart and put together. Polishes, lacquers, chemical cleansers, are not known merely as formulæ; but are actually made in small quantities by students themselves, so as to develop their power of doing things. Is this flour, bran, and baking powder, pure? Is the fertiliser of high grade? How shall the sick-room be disinfected? How shall we destroy the cabbage-devouring worm? To these and similar questions, the division of Chemistry seeks to enable students readily to find answers. In the course in Physics, the principles taken up are illustrated by the actual work going on in the outside building construction, and the farm work. Great stress is laid upon the bearing of Physics on tools, machines, and operations of the shops. Inspection of the various industrial plants in the vicinity of Tuskegee is required in order that the student may see the applications of Physics to the processes in use. Throughout the courses, a notebook is accurately kept by each student, in which are recorded the results of his observations and experiments, together with sketches for illustration.

An exercise given to one of the Junior classes in the night school, not long ago, shows how the attempt is made, even in so simple a matter as a spelling lesson, to correlate the Academic work with the Industrial.

The theme of this lesson was "Building a Chest," and the teacher brought to the class a small chest in which were placed most of the tools and materials needed in its construction. The teacher exhibited each article as he came to it in telling the story, and required the student to spell the word and then write it on the blackboard as neatly as possible. The synonyms and homonyms of some of the words were given, and the student required to illustrate their difference in spelling and use.

The teacher proceeded as follows, eliciting from the students the words in italics: To build this article we must have *Timber*, such as *Pine*, or *Cedar*, or *Cypress*, and other *Material*. We also need several *Tools*, such as a *Plane* to *Smooth* the *Planks;* a *Chisel* to cut these *Dove-tails;* and some *Glue*, with which to fasten the pieces together substantially, as we shall not need *Nails*. Then with these *Sprigs* we put on this *Moulding*, which should be cut in a *Miter*, or we may cut it by this *Bevel*, which can be changed to a *Square*. We now put on these *Butts*—not *Strap-Hinges*—with *Screws*. In front must be *Bored* a hole and the *Lock* put on; then the *Escutcheon* over the hole as a finish; the *Key* is inserted, and we have completed the *Chest*. A *Carpenter*—one engaged in *Carpentry*—or a *Cabinet-Maker*, builds things like this, and we call him a *Mechanic*.

The practical usefulness of the Academic Department lies in the aid which the study of physics and chemistry and mathematics and drawing offers to the blacksmith, the carpenter, the nurse, and the housewife—an aid that does much to transform listlessness and drudgery into vivacity and gratifying efficiency.

CHAPTER VIII

Lessons in Home-Making

WHILE the men must work to get and keep the home, the wives and daughters must, in a great measure, supply and guard the health, strength, morals, and happiness of the family. Their responsibility is great in all that makes for the development of the individual and the community. The home is built on an ancient foundation among the white population of this country, especially in the rural communities. The Negro has had to learn the meaning of home since he learned the meaning of freedom. All work which has to do with his uplifting must begin with his home and its surroundings.

Those familiar only with the rural life of the North and West, where, even in poverty, there are deep-grounded habits of thrift and comfort, do not know what home lacks among great masses of the cabin-dwellers of the South. Nowhere is there a nobler opportunity than that which confronts the young women who are learning at Hampton and Tuskegee, and other educational institutions, what home should be. The crowded one-room cabin affects the moral and physical life of the family, it slowly destroys the right inclinations given by nature to every child, and develops a manner of life which, coöperating with other causes, produces mental weakness, loss of ambition, and a shiftless disregard of responsibilities.

It goes without saying that many of the young women who come to Tuskegee need such training as will enable them to make homes that are worthy the name. It is the need first at hand, and the school tries to meet it in a practical way. The most liberal courses in literature and the sciences, if they exclude all practical training that will help a young woman to solve the problems which center around her own hearth, will not help her to get what she needs most.

At Tuskegee she is given a thorough English education, she can go out from the school and obtain a teacher's position in a· field where the demand is greater than the supply, but after all her duty begins at home, and it would be worse than folly to overlook these essentials. It is interesting to note, in this connection, that, after the household training system of Tuskegee had been in operation for some time, the need of similar education for young women whose natural advantages were infinitely greater than those of the coloured girls in the South, prompted the following announcement in the advertisement of what is, perhaps, the

most high-priced and exclusive seminary in Massachusetts:

"In planning a system of education for young
ladies, with the view of fitting them for the greatest
usefulness in life, the idea was conceived of supple-
menting the purely intellectual work by practical
training in the art of home management and its
related subjects.

"It was the first school of high literary grade to
introduce courses in Domestic Science into the
regular curriculum.

"The results were so gratifying as to lead to the
equipment of Experiment Hall, a special building,
fitted for the purpose of studying the principles
of Applied Housekeeping.   Here the girls do the
actual work of cooking, marketing, arranging
menus, and attend to all the affairs of a well-
arranged household.

"Courses are arranged also in sewing, dressmaking,
and millinery; they are conducted on a similar
practical basis, and equip the student with a thorough
knowledge of the subject."

A dozen years ago, I do not believe that any such
announcement would have been made.

At Tuskegee there is a modest dwelling of four
rooms, called the "practice cottage." In the
shadow of the massive brick buildings which sur-
round it, this cottage seems to have strayed in
from some one of the country roads around Tus-

LEARNING DRESSMAKING

kegee. But is has a trim and well-kept air, such as all country homes can have, no matter how poor and simple they may be. It contains a bedroom, sitting-room, dining-room and kitchen. These rooms are comfortably furnished for family house-keeping, but there is nothing in them that is not within reach of any Alabama farmer who is able to make both ends meet.

Much of the furniture is home-made. The creton-covered chairs, divan, and sofa are made from common barrels, which the girls are taught to make into furniture in the upholstering department. This kind of utility furniture has been so successful for ornament and comfort that a good deal of it has been ordered by visitors for their Northern homes. The floors of the cottage are covered with clean, cheap matting and oilcloth, and the students are taught to make pretty and serviceable mats from corn-husks. Whatever there is in the rooms is in good taste, for pictures, wall paper, and humble adornment can be worked out in good taste without extra cost.

The girls of the Senior class live in the "practice cottage" in turn, four at one time, for periods of five weeks. They are able to put into practice, under the supervision of Mrs. Washington, much that they have learned in their school life of three or four years. This is not, in reality, an "experiment station," for the girls are thoroughly equipped to

take charge of every department of the house, and
they run it themselves, being held responsible only
for results.

They do the sweeping, dusting, cooking, washing,
and ironing, sewing if need be, and their own marketing. The family of four is given an allowance of
not more than three dollars a week for food, which
they invest at the school store and the school farm.
With this allowance they are expected to set the
table for four, and to run their cuisine through the
week without any outside help. This seems a very
modest sum, but it is in fair proportion to the
average incomes of the class of people who need
just such training. The girls are thoroughly acquainted with the nutritive and appetising values
of the foods which will be available in their home
neighbourhoods.

Distinguished visitors have been guests of the
"practice cottage girls," and have enjoyed the
simple meals, skillfully prepared by the hostesses,
who make no extra preparations. On their small
allowance, and with the menu prepared in advance,
they are able to entertain without flurry or em-
barrassment. They have been taught that the
truest hospitality is in making the most of what one
has to do with, and offering no apologies for the
absence of luxuries one cannot afford. The "practice cottage" is well kept, and is an interesting
picture in miniature of the essentially practical

BARREL FURNITURE
A thriving Tuskegee industry

side of the school gospel of hard work with the hands as a part of a useful education.

Of course, this cottage routine is not allowed to interfere with the class work; and while they are testing their ability to manage a modest, clean, attractive, livable home, the girls are pursuing the studies they have selected to fit them for their several lines of work after graduation. In addition to the training in the Academic Department, these girls are learning trades, and, what is more important, how to make homes for themselves or for others. In this cottage the Senior girls round out their course by the practical application of all the theories in household economy that they have learned during the earlier years of their training. The course in "Domestic Science" is perhaps worth outlining in part because it is practical, and is designed to make the home an uplifting agency by its daily operation and influence:

First year: Making and care of fires; care and adjustment of lamps used for cooking; cleaning and keeping in order the tables, closets, sinks, and pantries; care of material as it comes from market; washing kitchen and cooking dishes, and care of baking-bowls, dish-towels, and dish-cloths; cleaning painted and unpainted woodwork; washing windows, sweeping and dusting; the proper use and care of utensils; making breads without yeast; making biscuit, corn-bread, sweet and white potato, graham and oatmeal bread; muffins of each of the flours, and combinations of rice or grits with them; making different kinds of toast and using stale breads; cooking vegetables in simple ways. The simplest forms of cooking meats; making plain, brown and milk gravies and sweet sauces; cooking cereals and serving in various ways; also cooking fish and eggs.

Second year: Care of silver, glass, china, brass and nickel; care of table linen; laying table for different meals, waiting, clearing table and washing dishes; cleaning oiled floors; lessons on providing material for meals, and calculating cost. Preparing given menus, and estimating time required in preparation; making yeast bread, brown and white, rolls, muffins, coffee, spice and raisin bread. Soup-making, with and without meat; purées from beans, peas and other vegetables, with or without milk; stews, hashes, minces. Cleaning and cooking chicken in various ways; bacon: boiled, fried. Making tea, chocolate, coffee and cocoa.

The third year deals with the theory of foods, their source, selection and composition and economic value, and the practice of principles involved in different methods of preparation.

The fourth and final year covers the study of dietaries, including the arrangment of bills of fare for daily living, in which the expense is limited to fifty cents for each person, and dinners of three courses for six persons.

In the school laundry the young women are taught the art of washing and ironing according to improved methods. Two washers, an extractor, a mangle, starcher, collar and cuff ironer, have been added to lighten the drudgery. Drying-rooms and ironing - rooms provided with excellent facilities afford means for thorough teaching. All of the washing for teachers and students, including bed and table linen, is done in this department. The course covers one school year.

It is the policy of the Institute to give special attention to the training of girls in all matters pertaining to dress, health, etiquette, physical culture and general housekeeping. The girls are constantly under the strict and watchful care of the Dean of the Woman's Department and the women teachers. Special rules governing the conduct of the girls are made known to each girl upon her arrival. In addition to the general training, they receive special practical talks from various members of the Faculty on such matters as relate to the care of the body, social purity, etc.

The course in household training includes such instruction as:—The location and sanitation of the home. Furniture: its purchase, arrangement, and proper care. Surroundings and their advantages. Cleaning: lamps, beds, bedrooms, and general weekly cleaning. The care of the dining-room: serving the table and the care of linen, silver, pantry, dishes, and towels. The duties and manners of the hostess. The furnishing and care of the kitchen. Marketing, and economy, punctuality, and regularity in preparation of food. The sick-room: its attractions and proper ventilation. Changing the patient's clothing and bedding. Feeding and visiting the sick. Yards and out-houses: how to keep clean and how to beautify. The housekeeper's personal appearance. Dress: what to wear and the colors suitable.

The hospital and training-school for nurses were organised to provide for the physical needs of the Tuskegee colony, and to equip young women for efficient service among their people. A beautiful two-story hospital building, with all modern improvements, has been finished, with enlarged facilities for the care of patients. The facilities for the training of nurses are excellent and the standard of admission high. Graduates from the hospital are doing good work, many of them holding excellent positions in the hospitals, schools and private infirmaries throughout the South. The five Tuskegee nurses sent to the front in the Spanish-American war were the only coloured female nurses employed by the Government. The course of study covers three years, but is so arranged that students of exceptional ability are able to complete it in two.

AN OUT-OF-DOOR CLASS IN LAUNDRY WORK
At the Mount Meig's School

CHAPTER IX

Outdoor Work for Women

Seven years ago I became impressed with the idea that there was a wider range of industrial work for our girls. The idea grew upon me that it was unwise in a climate like ours in the South to narrow the work of our girls, and confine them to indoor occupations.

If one makes a close study of economic conditions in the South, he will soon be convinced that one of the weak points is the want of occupations for women. This lack of opportunity grows largely out of traditional prejudice and because of lack of skill. All through the period of slavery, the idea prevailed that women, not slaves, should do as little work as possible with their hands. There were notable exceptions, but this was the rule.

Most of the work inside the homes was done by the coloured women. Such a thing as cooking, sewing, and laundering, as part of a white woman's education, was not thought of in the days of slavery. Training in art, music, and general literature was emphasised. When the coloured girl became free, she naturally craved the same education in which she had seen the white woman specialising. I have already described our trials at the Tuskegee Institute, in attempting to get our girls to feel and see that they should secure the most thorough education in everything relating to the care of a home. When we were able to free them of the idea that it was degrading to study and practice those household duties which are connected with one's life every day in the year, I felt convinced that one other step was necessary.

New England and most of the Middle States are largely engaged in manufacturing. The factories, therefore, naturally give employment to a large number of women. The South is not yet in any large degree manufacturing territory, but is an agricultural section and will probably remain such for a long period. This fact confirmed my belief that an industrial school should not only give training in household occupations to women, but should go further in meeting their needs and in providing education for them in out-of-door industries.

In making a study of this subject it became evident that the climate of every Southern State was peculiarly adapted to out-of-door work for women. A little later I had the opportunity of going to Europe and visiting the agricultural college for women at Swanley, England. There I found about forty women from some of the best families of Great Britain. Many of these women were graduates of high schools and colleges. In the morning I saw them in the laboratory and class room studying botany and chemistry and mathematics as applied to agriculture and horticulture. In the afternoon these same women were clad in suitable garments and at work in the field with the hoe or rake, planting vegetable seeds, pruning fruit trees or learning to raise poultry and bees and how to care for the dairy. After I had seen this work and had made a close study of it, I saw all the more clearly what should be done for the coloured girls of the South where there was so large an unemployed proportion of the population. I reasoned that if this kind of hand-training is necessary for a people who have back of them the centuries of English wealth and culture, it is tenfold more needful for a people who are in the condition of my race at the South.

I came home determined to begin the training of a portion of our women at Tuskegee in the outdoor industries. Mrs. Washington, who had made a careful study of the work in England, took charge of the outdoor work at Tuskegee. At first the girls were very timid. They felt ashamed to have any one see them at work in the garden or orchard. The young men and some of the women were inclined to ridicule those who were bold enough to lead off. Not a few became discouraged and stopped. There is nothing harder to overcome than an unreasonable prejudice against an occupation or a race. The more unreasonable it is, the harder it is to conquer. Mrs. Washington made a careful study of the girls and discovered the social leaders of a certain group. With this knowledge in hand she called the leaders together and had several conferences with them and explained in detail just what was desired and what the plans were. These leaders decided that they would be the pioneers in the outdoor work.

Beginning in a very modest way with a few girls, the outdoor work has grown from year to year, until it is now a recognised part of the work of the school, and the idea that this kind of labour is degrading has almost disappeared. In order to give, if possible, a more practical idea of just what is taught the girls, I give the entire course of study. In reading this it should be borne in mind that the theory is not only given, but in each case the girls have the training in actual work. Since the school year opens in the fall, the work naturally begins with the industries relating to the fall and winter. The course of study is:

First Year.—Fall Term.—Dairying.—The home dairy is first taken up, and a detailed knowledge of the following facts taught: Kinds, use and care of utensils, gravity, creaming. A study of stone, wooden, and tin churns, ripening of cream, churning, working and salting butter, preparation and marketing of same. Feeding and care of dairy cows.

Poultry Raising.—A working knowledge is required of the economic value of poultry on the farm, pure and mixed breeds, plain poultry-house construction, making of yards, nests, and runs.

Horticulture.—Instruction is given as to the importance of an orchard and small fruits, varieties best suited, particular locality, selection and preparation of ground, setting, trimming, extermination of borers, lice, etc., special stress being laid upon the quality and quantity of peaches, pears, apples, plums, figs, grapes, and strawberries that should be planted in a home orchard.

Floriculture and Landscape Gardening.—A study of our door-yards, how to utilise and beautify them. The kinds, care, and use of tools used in floriculture and landscape gardening. Trimming and shaping of beds and borders, and the general care of shrubbery and flowers. The gathering and saving of seed. Special treatment of rose bushes and shrubbery.

Market Gardening.—Importance of proper management of the home garden, its value to the home, selection and preparation of ground; kinds, care and use of tools, planting, gardening and marketing of all vegetables. Gathering of seeds, drying of pumpkins, okra, and fruits.

Live Stock.—Study is limited wholly to ordinary farm animals; the number and kind needed, how, when and what to feed; characteristics and utility of the various animals.

Winter Term.—Dairying.—The commercial dairy is the subject of study, and emphasis is laid upon the following: Use of separators, of which the school has two leading styles; churns, feeding, and care of the dairy herd, breeds of dairy cattle and their selection, butter-making, packing, salting and preparation for market.

Poultry Raising.—Special study of breeding and feeding. When, how and what kind of eggs and the breed of fowls to set; the period of incubation, poultry book-keeping, saving of eggs for market; an introductory of study of young chickens.

Floriculture and Landscape Gardening.—Trimming of beds and borders, mulching, tying, wrapping, and preparation of plants for the winter.

Winter decoration of grounds, the decorative value of native shrubbery; a study of window plants, their value in the home, halls and public buildings, their economic value, etc.

Market Gardening.—The selection of grounds and making of hotbeds, cold frames, etc., planting and managing of same, the raising of winter vegetables, marketing.

Spring Term.—Dairying.—Milking; a study of pastures, how to destroy lice and other parasites, the care of calves, the utilisation of waste in the dairy; laboratory work.

Poultry Raising.—A more advanced study of young poultry; brooders, sanitation of the house, runs, and of all the apparatus; egg-testing, moulting and its effects upon different breeds.

Horticulture.—Spring planting, trimming, budding, grafting, spraying, care of grape vines; the wire and post system of supports; spring layering and cuttings.

Floriculture and Landscape Gardening.—Renewing of beds and borders, seed sowing, special study of propagation by layers, cuttings, division of roots, bulbs, etc.; kinds and uses of fertilisers for this special season.

Market Gardening.—Preparation of ground, what and how to plant, special stress being laid upon the production of early vegetables for the home and market. Reproduction of plants by seeds and by division of numbers; water and its office in plant economy.

Live Stock.—Course includes the history, development, characteristics, standard points, utility, adaptability to climatic conditions; lessons on judging, care, selection and management of the leading breeds of horses, sheep and hogs.

Second Year.—Fall Term.—Dairying.—A more comprehensive study of milk and its constituents; weeds and their harmful effect upon dairy products; general sanitation of dairy barns; the drawing of plans, etc.

Poultry Raising.—Insecticides, how to make, when and how much to use, diseases of fowls and their treatment. A study of foods and their adaptability to different breeds, special study of turkeys and guineas.

Horticulture.—Root and stem grafting with active and dormant buds; formation of trunk and top starch, and its relation to the hardiness of fruits and shrubs, botany of the orchard, entomology; bookkeeping.

Floriculture and Landscape Gardening.—Systematic botany, bouquet-making—harmony of colour, form and size of flowers; laying out of private and public grounds, roads, parks, walks, and streets; entomology of the flower garden.

Market Gardening.—Botany of the field and garden; physical analysis of soils and the improvement of clay and sandy soils; the depletion of plant food and its replacement by direct and indirect fertilisers; the source of carbon, nitrogen and oxygen. Draining.

Live Stock.—How to hitch and unhitch horses, the care of vehicles and harness, how to drive, the names of common diseases and treatment of sick animals; swine for profit.

Winter Term. — Dairying. — The weighing and recording of milk in a commercial dairy; the Babcock and other methods of testing milk; composition of cheese and its value as a food.

Poultry Raising.—Composition of the animal body; a special study of ducks and geese; brooders, ponds, runs, etc., by-products and their value.

Horticulture.—Forestry, botany, cryptogamic and systematic; nut culture; preservation of timber, the economic value of different woods; the relation of forests to climate, water supply, floods and erosion.

Market Gardening.—A study of the life-history of insects, injuries to stored grain, peas, beans, meal, flour, dried fruits; botany of the greenhouse, cold frame and hotbeds; the use of thermometers. A study of markets, library work.

Spring Term.—Dairying.—Cottage and Chedder cheese-making, scoring of butter, bacteriology of milk, butter, and cheese. Judging of dairy animals by the score-card method, diseases of cows and their treatment; analysis of food stuffs.

Poultry Raising.—Physical and chemical study of foods, library work, fancy breeds, what and how to exhibit, the history and development of the industry. Heredity and the effects of in-breeding.

Horticulture.—Origin of new varieties by cross-fertilisation, hybrids, sports, atavisms and reversion, correlation between plants and animals, rejuvenating by pruning, grafting and scraping the bark, special diseases of both trees and fruit, and their treatment. Knot-growth, blight, gum excrescences and frost injuries; drying, preserving, making fruit syrups, etc.

Horticulture and Landscape Gardening.—Special designing in cultivated flowers. Origin of new species; bees and their relation to the forest and garden; the hiving of bees and after-management. A study of honey-producing plants; the economic value of the honey.

Market Gardening.—Relation of crops, geology of the garden, agricultural chemistry, good roads and their relation to the success and value of the farm, mineralogy and useful birds and insects.

I believe that all who will make a careful study of the subject will agree with me that there is a vast unexplored field for women in the open air. The South, with its mild climate and other advantages, is as well adapted to out-door labour for women as to that for men. There is not only an advantage in material welfare, but there is the advantage of a superior mental and moral growth. The average woman who works in a factory becomes little more than a machine. Her planning and thinking is done for her. Not so with the woman who depends upon raising poultry, for instance, for a living. She must plan this year for next, this month for the next. Naturally there is a growth of self-reliance, independence, and initiative.

Life out in the sweet, pure, bracing air is better from both a physical and a moral point of view than long days spent in the close atmosphere of a factory or store. There is almost no financial risk to be encountered, in the South, in following the occupations which I have enumerated. The immediate demands for the products of garden, dairy, poultry yard, apiary, orchard, etc., are pressing and ever present. The satisfaction and sense of independence that will come to a woman who is brave enough to follow any of these outdoor occupations infinitely surpass the results of such uncertain labor as that of peddling books or cheap jewelry, or similar employments, and I believe that a larger number of our schools in the near future will see the importance of outdoor handwork for women.

There is considerable significance in the fact that this year more than fifty girls have taken up the study of scientific farming at the Minnesota College of Agriculture, and have thus announced their intention to adhere to country life. The college has been in existence for the past decade, but girls have only recently been admitted. The character of the instruction available to the girl students is suggestive. The course presented emphasises the sciences of botany, chemistry, physics and geology, requiring, during the freshman and sophomore years at least, two terms' work in each of them. Boys and girls work together throughout two-thirds of the entire course, which includes study in language, mathematics, science, civics, and considerable technical work. In the courses for girls, cooking, laundering and sewing are substituted for carpentry, blacksmithing and veterinary science. The girls, too, give more attention to household art, home economy and domestic hygiene than to the business aspect of farming. It is happily the chief purpose of the college to awaken in its entire student body a keen interest in farming, farm life, the farm-house and farm society. Both boys and girls are taught to plan farm buildings and to lay out the grounds artistically. Considerable attention is given to the furnishing of houses, to literature, music and social culture, with the general thought of making the farm home the most attractive spot on earth. The result of the new movement is being watched with keen interest by agriculturists and educators. It is evident that, should it prove successful, the innovation will spread to other agricultural States. Its influence, one readily apprehends, is apt to be social as well as agricultural in character. Heretofore, one great drawback to farming, even in the North, has been the difficulty of keeping the farmers' sons on the farm. With trained and educated girls enthusiastically taking up the profession of farming, the country life will take on new charms, and the exodus of young men to cities will be materially lessened.

CHAPTER X

HELPING THE MOTHERS

SOMETHING about the Woman's Meeting, organised and conducted in the town of Tuskegee by Mrs. Washington, seems not out of place in this book. It is her work, and she has kindly supplied the following outline of the aims and results of this attempt to better the conditions and lives of the people living in this typical Alabama community:

In the spring of '92, the first Negro Conference for farmers was held at Tuskegee. The purpose of this conference was to inspire the masses of coloured people to secure homes of their own, to help them to better ways of living, to insist upon better educational advantages for them, and so to raise their standards of living, morally, physically, intellectually and financially. Sitting in that first meeting of Negro farmers and hearing the resolutions which stood as the platform of the conference, I felt that history was repeating itself. In the days of Lucretia Mott, and the early struggles of Susan B. Anthony, women had no rights that were worth mentioning, and, notwithstanding the fact that

there were many women present at this first conference, they had little actual place in it.

Perhaps they did not realise that they, too, had
a most prominent part to play in the life which their
lovers, or their sons and husbands, were urged to
seek.   Perhaps they did not dream that they would
some day have a vital part in the uplifting of our
people.   This thought would not be stilled: What
can these poor farmers do with the new ideas, new
hopes, new aspirations, unless the women can be
equally inspired and interested in conferences of
their own?

Not many days passed before there was a fixed
purpose in my mind that these women in the homes
represented by the farmers should be reached.
How to reach and help them was the question.
After many weary days and sleepless nights, praying
for some way to open, the thought came that the
village of Tuskegee was a good place to begin work.
The country women, tired of the monotony of
their lives, came crowding into the village every
Saturday.   There should be a place for them to go
to be instructed for an hour or more each Saturday.
Like a flash the idea was caught up, and it was not
let go until such a place was secured.

Our first conference was held in the upper story
of a very dilapidated store which stands on the main
street of the village.   The stairs were so rickety
that we were often afraid to ascend them.   The

room was used by the coloured firemen of the village, and was a dark and dreary place, uninviting even to me. It answered our purpose for the time. We had no rent to pay, and that was one less burden for us. How to get the women to the first meeting was not easily settled. For fear of opposition from friends, no mention had been made of the plan, except to the man who let me have the room.

That first Saturday I walked up the stairs alone, and sat down in the room with all its utter dreariness. My heart almost failed me, and not until I remembered these words: "No man, having put his hand to the plow and looking back, is fit for the Kingdom of God," did I throw off the despondency. At this moment a small boy entered the room. I said to him, "Go through the streets and say to each woman, so that no one else will hear you, there is a woman up those stairs who has something for you."

That first meeting I can never forget. There were six women who came, and each one as she looked at me seemed to say: "Where is it?" We talked it all over, the needs of our women, the best ways of helping each other, and there was begun the first woman's weekly conference, which now numbers nearly three hundred women.

We now have a large, roomy hall on the main street, where we come together each Saturday, and spend two hours talking of the things which go to make better and truer lives among women and children. Women come long distances on foot to these meetings. They soon brought with them their little girls, whom they could not afford to leave at home, and there arose a new question—what to do with the children? A plan was hit upon, and a room hired. These girls, now more than fifty in number, are taught simple lessons, and, at the same time, receive short practical talks on behaviour at home, on the streets and elsewhere. We also have a small library for them, and each one is allowed to draw the books she wants, to keep two weeks or longer. We also have picture books on the table for the younger children. We are now trying to get games for these children and pictures for the walls of the room. A friend gives two hours of her time on Saturday to these children, and it delights one's heart to see the improvement in them in all directions, especially in their quiet and becoming conduct on the streets.

The marked improvement among the women in the matter of dress has been frequently commented upon in the village. They are doing away with the wrapping of the hair, and substituting for it braiding or some other simple arrangement. The women no longer go barefooted, nor do they sit around the streets in a listless way. There is less familiarity among the men and women in the streets, and in many ways the women are being led into better ways of conduct, to say nothing of home improvements and the closer union of family life.

We visit the homes of the women and see that the lessons are put into practice. We have given out thousands of papers and picture cards, that the cracks might be closed against the wind and rain, and that the children of the home might have something besides the dark and cheerless logs to look at.

Soon the women began to see the importance of these conferences, and to do all in their power to promote their interests. Our talks were discussed on the farms and in neighbourhood chat. Their influence spread in indirect channels. These talks were planned along such simple and practical lines as the following subjects suggest:

Morals among young girls.

The kinds of amusements for young girls.

A mother's example.

A mother's duty to her home.

Dresses for women and children.

Poultry raising for women.

The part a woman should take in securing a home.

Fruit canning, etc.

Many other subjects were suggested by the women themselves, and afterward put in written form so that they could read them intelligently. Many of the talks were grouped in a little book for women who could not reach the conferences. These books contain also little recipes which any woman may need in her country home, especially when there is sickness in the family. Work for the masses is always more difficult than for the individual, but it is work which must be done. Eighty per cent. of our women have their homes in the country or on the plantations, they live in the old-time log cabins, but they have hearts, they have aspirations for the future. In pursuance of the ideas which prompted this humble crusade, I have sent out leaflets which embody, among others, these suggestions for teachers and other workers, which I have found exceedingly helpful in organising home-union meetings for mothers:

Decide upon a definite time for holding a meeting, and then send notice to the mothers by the school children.

Once every three or six months have a general meeting with simple refreshments such as can be gotten in a country village.

Now and then an experience meeting can be held to the advantage of all. Encourage the women to talk freely of their own plans.

Find out by judicious visiting whether any advancement is made.

Do not expect too much in a short time, and, above all, do not be dictatorial while visiting, or personal in meetings when you wish to deal with mistakes that you have seen in the homes visited.

Some Subjects for Talks

How to keep home neat and tidy.

How to make home attractive for husband and children.

Amusements, music and reading in the home circle.

Is it necessary to teach the girls to do good by teaching them how to do housework, cooking and sewing?

The relations of mothers to their children.

How to gain the confidence of children.

How to correct falsehood and theft among boys and girls.

Is there not a share in the home for the boys?

How to teach boys and men to respect women generally by teaching them to respect mothers and sisters.

The mother's authority in selecting company for her sons and daughters.

When should a girl be allowed to receive company? How can a mother help her to avoid mistakes as regards the young man she loves?

What part should a woman take with her husband in securing a home or a piece of land on which to build one?

What is the effect upon the face when the hair is

wrapped with coloured strings? Why not plat it or arrange it in some other becoming way?

Should women go barefooted?

Love of gaudy dress for children. What will the result be when they are older and cannot afford to buy the same sort?

Manners on the street.

Necessity of varying diet for the household.

Economy in the house as regards food.

The proper duty of mothers in having the family table set with care at the proper time.

The importance of ventilation, proper food, and cleanliness of body on the moral atmosphere of the home.

What lessons can be drawn from Thanksgiving Day, New Year's and Christmas?

The mother's relation to the church and the minister.

How the family should go to church. Isn't it better if all go together and sit together, too?

How can boys and girls be taught the habit of giving to the church and charitable purposes?

How may mothers and their daughters best resist men who attempt to rob them of their honour and virtue?

The best way to inspire children to purity of thought, speech, and action, at home and abroad?

In a leaflet of practical help, for these mothers' meetings, some of the simple teachings are put in detail form, and these may give an idea of what we are trying to do in these directions, and what are the common needs of the people among whom we are working. Under the head of "Your Needs" are the following items:

You need chairs in your houses. Get boxes. Cover them with bright calico, and use them for seats until you can buy chairs. You need plates, knives and forks, spoons and table-cloths. Buy them with tobacco and snuff money.

You need more respect for self. Get it by staying away from street corners, depots, and, above all, excursions. You need to stay away from these excursions to keep out of bad company, out of court, out of jail, and out of the disgust of every self-respecting person.

You need more race pride. Cultivate this as you would your crops. It means a step forward. You need a good home. Save all you can. Get your own home, and that will bring you nearer citizenship. You can supply all these needs. When will you begin? Every moment of delay is loss.

How to Become Prosperous

Keep no more than one dog. Stay away from court. Buy no snuff, whisky and tobacco. Raise your own pork. Raise your own vegetables. Put away thirty cents for every dollar you spend.

Get a good supply of poultry. Set your hens.

Keep your chickens until they will bring a good price.

Go to town on Thursday instead of Saturday. Buy no more than you need.

Stay in town no longer than necessary.

My Daily Work

I may take in washing, but every day I promise myself that I will do certain work for my family. I will set the table for every meal. I will wash the dishes after every meal.

Monday I will do my family washing. I will put my bedclothes out to air. I will clean the food closet with hot water and soap.

Tuesday I will do my ironing and family patching.

Wednesday I will scrub my kitchen, and clean my yard thoroughly.

Thursday I will clean and air the meal and pork boxes. I will scour my pots and pans with soap and ashes.

Friday I will wash my dish-cloth, dish-towels, and hand-towels. I will sweep and dust my whole house, and clean everything thoroughly.

Saturday I will bake bread, cake, and do other extra cooking for Sunday. I will spend one hour in talking with my children, that I may know them better.

Sunday I will go to church and Sunday School. I will take my children with me. I will stay at home during the remainder of the day. I will try to read aloud a something helpful to all.

QUESTIONS I WILL PLEDGE MYSELF TO ANSWER AT THE END OF THE YEAR

How many bushels of potatoes, corn, beans, and peanuts have we raised this year?

How many hogs and cows do we keep? How much poultry have we raised? How many bales of cotton have we raised? How much have we saved to buy a home?

How much have we done toward planting flowers and making our yard look pretty? How many kinds of vegetables did we raise in our home garden?

How many times did we stay away from miscellaneous excursions when we wished to go? What were our reasons for staying at home? Have we helped our boys and girls to stay out of bad company? What paper have we taken, and have we taken our children to church and had them sit with us?

The experiment of real settlement work on a plantation near Tuskegee was begun in 1896 in a dilapidated, unused one-room cabin in the quarters of the "big house," where resided the last scion of a family of slave-holders.

Seventy-five families lived scattered in cabins over the two-thousand-acre plantation in easy access to their plots of land farmed on shares. Many of the men were paying for "time" bought by the owner of the plantation. Some had been arrested, and on trial found guilty. They had to pay either a certain sum or suffer imprisonment. The owner of the plantation paid the fines, and the men paid him for their time in labour. Schools were miles distant, and the only opportunity to teach the better way of life seemed to be establishing a settlement. The planter graciously granted the free use of the cabin aforesaid. Students from the Institute nailed the shingles on the open roof. The room was given a thorough cleaning, and in a short time a young woman graduate, now wife of the Principal of Christianburg Institute, Cambria, Virginia, and an undergraduate moved in with her home-made furniture—fashioned from dry-goods boxes, and covered with pretty chintz sent by an old friend who has now passed to her reward.

As a Sunday School had begun in one of the log houses several Sundays previous to the opening of the settlement, the young teacher's coming had been explained, and all had promised to contribute all they could to her support.

The first articles of food entered on the teacher's book to the credit of her patrons were two eggs, one can of syrup, one half-pound bacon, one quart meal, one can buttermilk. The teacher cooked her meals on her oven in the fireplace, did her work, and taught school in her cabin. The first day brought fifteen

HOME-MADE FURNITURE

boys and girls. Ten of the fathers and mothers, eager to learn how to read and write, came to the night school. For two years the teacher struggled. Her patrons helped her with larder, and grew— measuring up to the standards of true living.

In spite of frequent patchings, the teacher's cabin became almost unfit for use. There came a time when umbrellas were indispensable in the cabin during a heavy downpour. In 1898 a way opened for the purchase of ten acres of woodland. A two-room cottage was built for the teacher on a clearing. No prouder workers could be found than the teacher and her pupils in clearing the land for possible crops. Beginning with 1900, the average annual yield was as follows: Two bales of cotton, forty bushels of corn, seventy-five bushels sweet potatoes, twenty bushels peanuts, twenty bushels pease, four loads shucks and fodder, greens, cabbage, and other vegetable products.

Two years ago a kitchen was added to the cottage, and the cooking classes of the school arose to the dignity of having a real stove and other necessaries. Sewing, cooking, gardening, and housekeeping classes have succeeded wonderfully. The boys of the settlement have received first prizes from Tuskegee Institute Agricultural Fair for their products put on exhibition.

One of the first fruits of the settlement work has been the promotion of a boy from that school to

Tuskegee Institute.   He has stood the test of four years in his classes, industrial and academic, and is now most promising.

The second step to place the work on a hopeful basis has been the purchase of ten more acres of land.   A two-room cottage has been built recently, and the mother of the first settlement boy to come to the front, and one of our pioneer workers in the venture, has been given a chance to not only earn her living, but to serve as a native object-lesson of neatness in her home and surroundings.   Eight years of constant work teaching old and young how to live has resulted in better built homes on the plantation.   Owner has replaced one-room log cabins with two-room cottages.

House to house visits and the object-lesson of the settlement work have told for good in the matter of cleanliness.   The marriage tie is respected.   It is the exception rather than the rule to find unmarried mothers living with their children's fathers without even a sense of shame.

The barefoot boys and girls, men and women, who first attended the settlement Sunday School eight years ago, come neatly dressed.   Men and women who could not read or write in the beginning of the work can read their Sunday School lessons and write a presentable note in a matter of business.

The Mothers' Union has brought the mothers to see the deep necessity of exerting their influence for good of home and people. The penny savings bank held by the teacher represents stockholders that mean to be owners of their own homes.

In the night school, the grown people, who are employed during the day, are taught the simple lessons which were neglected in their youth. At first many of them were ashamed to admit their ignorance. One young man, whom Mrs. Washington noticed during one of her visits as being particularly sullen when asked to join the class, has turned out to be one of the most ambitious pupils. "At first I was almost afraid to speak to him," she said, "but after I talked to him a little while, he broke down quite suddenly, and exclaimed:

"Oh, Mis' Washington! I'se so ashamed, I don't even know my letters." But it is the classes in cooking and cleaning and sewing which have been most successful, and these are responsible more than anything else for the change in the women.

From the outset, the white planters who employ most of the coloured families of the settlement have aided in the work. When Mrs. Washington first sent for permission to carry on some missionary work among his tenants, he sent a boy on a mule with a fat turkey, and a message for me to "come and do anything I liked." What seemed to be a discouragement at first was that occasionally a family moved away, thus causing the teacher to begin all over again, with a newcomer, the work which had been scarce finished with the old.   Later she came to see that those who migrated served to spread the influence into other neighbourhoods, thus broadening the teachings far beyond her own limitations.

CHAPTER XI

THE TILLERS OF THE GROUND

THERE is held at the Tuskegee Institute every year a remarkable conference of Negro workers, mostly farmers, who are to work out their salvation by the sweat of their brows in tilling the soil of the South. The purpose of these gatherings is severely practical—to encourage those who have not had the advantages of training and instruction, and to give them a chance to learn from the success of others as handicapped as they what are their own possibilities. As I have said many times, it is my conviction that the great body of the Negro population must live in the future as they have done in the past, by the cultivation of the soil, and the most hopeful service now to be done is to enable the race to follow agriculture with intelligence and diligence.

I have just finished reading a little pamphlet written by Mr. George W. Carver, Director of the Agricultural Department at Tuskegee, giving the results of some of his experiments in raising sweet potatoes for one year. This coloured man has shown in plain, simple language, based on scientific principles, how he has raised two hundred and sixty-six bushels of sweet potatoes on a single acre of common land, and made a net profit of one hundred and twenty-one dollars. The average yield of sweet potatoes to the acre, in the part of the South where this experiment was tried, is thirty-seven bushels per acre. This coloured man is now preparing to make this same land produce five hundred bushels of potatoes.

I have watched this experiment with a great deal of pleasure. The deep interest shown by the neighbouring white farmers has been most gratifying. I do not believe that a single white farmer who visited the field to see the unusual yield ever thought of having any prejudice or feeling against this coloured man because his education had enabled him to make a marked success of raising sweet potatoes. There were, on the other hand, many evidences of respect for this coloured man and of gratitude for the information which he had furnished.

If we had a hundred such coloured men in each county in the South, who could make their education felt in meeting the world's needs, there would be no race problem. But in order to get such men, those interested in the education of the Negro must begin to look facts and conditions in the face. Too great a gap has been left between the Negro's real condition and the position for which we have tried to fit him through the medium of our text-books. We have overlooked in many cases the fact that long years of experience and discipline are necessary for any race

before it can get the greatest amount of good out of
the text-books. Much that the Negro has studied
presupposes conditions that do not, for him, exist.

The weak point in the past has been that no
attempt has been made to bridge the gap between the
Negro's educated brain and his opportunity for sup-
plying the wants of an awakened mind. There has
been almost no thought of connecting the educated
brain with the educated hand. It is almost a crime to
take young men from the farm, or from farming districts, and educate them, as is too often done, in
everything except agriculture, the one subject with
which they should be most familiar. The result is
that the young man, instead of being educated to
love agriculture, is educated out of sympathy with it;
and instead of returning to his father's farm after
leaving college, to show him how to produce more
with less labour, the young man is often tempted to
go into the city or town to live by his wits.

The purpose of the Tuskegee Negro Conference is
to help the farmers who are too old, or too bound
down by their responsibilities, to attend schools or
institutes; to do for them, in a small way, what Tuskegee and other agencies seek to do for the younger
generation. Coloured men and women make long and
expensive journeys to be present, coming from all
the Southern and several of the Northern states.
They have found that their money is not wasted, for
they learn much by seeing what has been done at the

school, from the advice of experts, but more especially by the exchange of opinions and by comparing experiences in their own field of work. These meetings are not for whining or complaints. Their keynote is hopeful courage. To look up and not down, forward and not backward, to be cheerful and mutually helpful, is the golden rule of the conference.

It was decided from the first to confine the proceedings to matters which the race had closely within its own control, and to positive, aggressive effort, rather than to mere negative criticisms and recitations of wrongs. I wanted these coloured farmers and their wives to consult about the methods and means of securing homes, of freeing themselves from debt, of encouraging intelligent production, of paying their taxes, of cultivating habits of thrift, honesty and virtue, of building school-houses, and securing education and high Christian character, of cementing the friendships between the races.

In these conventions, as in other ways, we have tried to keep alive the feeling of hope and encouragement. We have seen darker days than these, and no race that is patient, long-suffering, industrious, economical, and virtuous, no race that is persistent in efforts that make for progress, no race that cultivates a spirit of good-will toward all mankind, is left without reward.

The Farmers' Conference each year adopts a

declaration of principles, which sum up its objects in such words as these:

"Our object shall be to promote the moral, material, and educational progress of this entire community. Believing, as we do, that we are our own worst enemies, we pledge, here and now, from this time forth, to use every effort—

"To abolish and do away with the mortgage system just as rapidly as possible.

"To raise our food supplies, such as corn, potatoes, syrup, pease, hogs, chickens, etc., at home rather than to go in debt for them at the store.

"To stop throwing away our time and money on Saturdays by standing around towns, drinking and disgracing ourselves in many other ways.

"To oppose, at all times, the excursion and camp-meeting, and to try earnestly to secure better schools, better teachers, and better preachers.

"To try to buy homes, to urge upon all Negroes the necessity of owning homes and farms, and not only to own them, but to beautify and improve them.

"Since the greater number of us are engaged in agriculture, we urge the importance of stock and poultry raising, the teaching of agriculture in the country schools, the thorough cultivation of a small acreage, rather than the poor cultivation of a large one, attention to farm-work in winter, and getting rid of the habit of living in one-room houses.

"We urge more protection to life and property, better homes for tenants, and that home life in the country be made more attractive, all this with the view of keeping such great numbers of our people out of the large cities.

"In connection with the better schools and churches, we emphasise the need of careful attention to the morals of our ministers and teachers, and all others acting in the capacity of leaders.

"Prosperity and peace are dependent upon friendly relations between the races, and to this end we urge a spirit of manly forbearance and mutual interest."

What these conferences are doing, and what sort of people are coming to them every year, may be gathered from some of their experiences as they have told them themselves during their visit to Tuskegee. Some of the best things are said by men and women who have succeeded in working their way up from abject poverty to comfortable independence. There is no better antidote for the foolish talk so often heard about the inevitable shiftlessness of the Negro race than these short and pithy narratives of sacrifice, struggle and achievement. A Florida man said that he had six dollars when he married. He now owns two hundred acres and a home of seven rooms. "I did without most everything until I got it paid for," he explained. He has fifty-seven head of cattle, six work horses, and five colts, all raised by himself.

Is it dangerous to give the ballot to that kind of a citizen? Will he be apt to use it to promote extravagant taxation?

An Alabama farmer said:

"I own sixty-seven acres of land. I got it by working hard and living close. I did not eat at any big tables. I often lived on bread and milk. I have five rooms to my house. I started with one, and that was made of logs. I add a room every year. I was lucky in marrying a woman whose father gave her a cow. I ain't got no fine clock or organ. I did once own a buggy, but it was a shabby one, and now we ride in a wagon, or I go horse-back on a horse I raised that is worth two hundred and fifty dollars. I have seven children in school."

"I started plowing with my pants rolled up and barefoot," said a Georgia man. "I saved five hundred dollars and bought a home in Albany, Georgia. I bought two hundred acres for seven dollars an acre, and paid for it in three years. I made that pay for two hundred acres more. After awhile I bought thirteen hundred acres. I live on it, and it is all paid for. I have twenty-five buildings and they all came out of my pocketbook. That land is now worth twenty-five dollars an acre. For a distance of four or five miles from my settlement, there has not been a man in the chain-gang for years. I work forty-seven head of mules. The only way we will ever be a race is by getting homes and living a virtuous life. I don't give mortgages. I take mortgages on black and white. I have put the first bale of cotton on the market in Georgia every year for eight years."

A widow from Alabama told her story, which shows among other things how a dog may be useful:

"There are three in my family, and I am the boss. I save about a hundred dollars a year. I give no mortgages. I plant everything that a farmer can plant. I raise my own syrup, meat, pease, corn, and everything we need to eat. I have three cows. You have got to go low down to get up high. I traded a little puppy with my brother for a pig. From this one pig I raised eight pigs, and for seven years I have not bought a pound of meat. I am living on the strength of that little puppy yet. I own forty acres, and sometimes rent more land."

A coloured minister from Alabama said that he farmed as well as preached. He was a renter for seven years. In nine years he paid for four hundred acres, and now owns ten hundred and fifteen acres. He raises horses, cows, mules, and hogs and has fifty persons dependent upon him. He owns the land where he used to live as a renter, and lives in the house of the man from whom he rented. There are few white people in his neighbourhood. Most of the coloured people own their own homes, and they have lengthened the annual school term two months at their own expense. This man said that, when he first bought land, he split rails to fence it during the day and carried them around at night, and his wife built the fence.

A South Carolinian, who was never before so far from home, said that he was a slave for twenty years. "I used to work six days for my master, and Sunday for myself," he said. "God introduced ten commandments, but our people have added another, 'Thou shalt not work Saturdays or Sundays, either.' I stick to the Ten Commandments and put in six days a week, and in that way have bought three hundred acres and paid for it. I have a large house for my own family of ten, and fourteen other buildings on the place, six of them rented. No man is a farmer excepting the man who lives on the produce of his farm."

A visitor from Louisiana told how he had borrowed two hundred and fifty dollars from his father and bought twenty-five acres of land in 1877. He used to begin work at four o'clock in the morning. For a year his wife ground all their meal, three ears at a time, in a small hand-mill. Now he owns three hundred acres of sugar land, worth a hundred dollars an acre, and has twenty-seven white and forty-eight coloured people working for him.

"I would like to set a big table for you," said one of these farmers whom I visited at his home, "but, professor, you-all is teachin' us to 'conermise an' save, an' dats what I'se tryin' to do," When you remember how anxious the good farmers and their wives are always to set a good table for the visiting "professors" and "revrums," this man had a good deal of courage in departing from old customs.

I say to the farmers: "If feeding the 'brutherins' is a strain on you, feed no more of them. Cut down on all expenses that can be trimmed without injury to yourself."

One woman from Bullock County, Alabama, carried away the true spirit of the conference. Not long ago, one of our agents saw a deed to a valuable piece of farm land, bought with money she had saved by selling cows. She said that she had never thought of any such plan until she had visited the Farmers' Conference and heard others tell how they had bought land. An unusual feature of this case was that the woman did not live in the town in which she had invested her money. She had made herself interested enough to seek a chance to invest her earnings in the purchase of property several miles from her home settlement. She said that it required a mighty sight of will-power to keep from buying fine clothes with the money, but she was determined to get hold of some land, and she did it without any assistance from her husband.

"Yes, of course I'll be at the next Negro Conference," wrote another farmer, "I want you to give me a chance to talk, too. I want to show Mr. Washington a turnip I raised in my own garden, and have been saving for the Conference, and I want to tell him how much I have raised and eaten out of my own garden, and how much I have saved as the result of these teachings at the annual meetings."

Another wrote recently:

"I have to buy very little to eat, for I raise with one horse all I want to eat, and a little more besides. Last year I raised nine bales of cotton, plenty of corn, sugar cane, pease, and potatoes, and many other things. Besides this, my wife raised twenty hogs, and a yard full of chickens, geese and turkeys. The only way for the farmer to get out of debt and keep out of debt is to buy a home, raise what he eats, and pay at once for what he gets out of the store."

A pilgrim from Georgia thus expressed himself:

"I came here to get my keg full of good news and glad tidings to carry back to Georgia, and I have got it. I began working for myself when I was eighteen years old. My father and mother died when I was a child. I first worked for eight dollars and fifty cents a month and my board, and cleared eighty-three dollars the first year. Then I worked on shares for a while, then I bought a mule on credit, using my money to support myself while raising a crop. Now I own fifteen hundred acres of land, all paid for. I have six rooms in my house. I don't give any mortgages. I have twenty-three plows, and a bank account. I haul on my drays about ten thousand bales of cotton every year for the planters in my county. I have another patch of fifty acres near Fort Gaines on which there is a six-room house."

"We come here to learn wisdom and knowledge," said a man from Macon County, Alabama. "I had a part of the slavery time, and I've had all of the freedom time. When I was in my eighteenth year I wanted to marry the worst way. I did it somehow, and then we tried every plan to get ahead in the world. I worked Sunday as well as Monday. I even hitched myself to the plow, and my wife plowed me. Now I have got horses, mules, corn, and plenty of everything to do me, but I have not got any home. Next year when I come here I am going to own a place of my own instead of renting it."

Scores of similar illustrations could be quoted to show that the Negro farmer is fighting his own battles, and that in his annual visits to Tuskegee he preaches, both to the students and to his fellow toilers, the gospel of work with the hands as the pathway to freedom. The kind of practical advice distributed among these farmers is illustrated in the following specimen of the leaflets issued by our "Bureau of Nature Study for Schools." This one on Hints and Suggestions for Farmers has to do with the ever-vital question of "Mortgage Lifting":

"Farmers all over the Cotton Belt are now finishing their plans for the growing of this year's crop. All sorts of financial plans have been made. Perhaps the most common among our farmers is the credit plan or crop mortgage. In this the farmer binds himself and family to make a crop, usually cotton, for any one who will 'advance' him what he must buy while growing the crop. He agrees to pay interest, ranging from ten to thirty-five per cent. on the cost of the things furnished. Thus a pair of shoes which would sell for $1.50 in cash would cost about $2 in the fall. If allowed to run until the next Fall, it would cost him about $2.50. If allowed to run three years, it would take $3.15 to pay for a $1.50 pair of shoes. If carried the fourth year, it would take $4, and one year more would call for $5.

"Too many farmers are paying $5 for shoes which would have cost them only $1.50 if they had managed their business properly. Too many times the $5 shoes are never paid for, leaving an unkindly feeling between the 'advancer' and the one 'advanced,' causing the landlord and tenant, and very often the merchant, to suffer.

"Yet the farmer must have clothing. He must have plows, hoes, wagons, etc. No man who tills the soil should have to suffer for something to eat. Perhaps no one will question the farmer's right to make the crop mortgage. He must and ought to have plenty of good, wholesome food to make it possible for him to do his work well. But for his own good, the good of his family, for the good of the landlord, and the community in which he lives, we do dispute his right to manage business as many of our farmers do. He should not make a mortgage he cannot easily lift.

"If it requires $150 to supply a farmer for a season, at the end of that season his debt will be about $180— an extra $30, the average value of a bale of cotton, to do a credit business. If it requires $75 to carry him, he will owe about $90, costing him half a bale of cotton to do a credit business. Now, do you note that the smaller the amount borrowed, the smaller the amount of interest, and the easier it becomes for the farmer to lift the whole thing? Don't load so heavily. Put two thousand pounds on a thousand-pound wagon and see what becomes of you, your load, and your wagon. One man tries by main strength to lift a large load. He fails and gives up in despair. Another man gets a long pole, or lever, and with the greatest ease raises and places the load where it is wanted. The first uses only muscle, while the last mixes muscle with brains.

"Could we not say the same thing of the unsuccessful and the successful mortgage lifter? If you will use your head and go at that debt in the right way, you will be surprised with what great ease you can get it out of the way. Well, how can this be done, one man asks? What would you advise? A wise man listens to advice. If he thinks it good, he will try to follow it. The farmer who is in debt must—

"Not make bad bargains. He must work all day

and sometimes part of the night, and buy only what he is compelled to have. He should raise everything he eats and a little more, and then cultivate as much cotton as he can.

"Some of the farmers buy shoddy goods at fair prices. They allow the boys and girls to buy cheap jewelry. They buy a sewing machine on credit for fifty or sixty dollars, and when they get it paid for, if they ever do, it has cost about a hundred dollars. They pay ten and fifteen dollars for a washstand and bureau when an upholstered box would do for the present. The industrious farmer works from sunrise to sunset every day in the week. If there is some light work he can do by putting in two or three hours during the long winter nights, you find him at it. It takes this to lift the mortgage.

"The sensible farmer will not buy five hundred pounds of bacon if there is any way to get along with two hundred and fifty. If he must buy it on credit, he will eat butter, drink milk, raise and eat eggs and chickens, kill a young beef when he can, and dry or pickle it, so as to supply his wants from his own produce as long as possible.

"The farmer who wants to get out of debt will have large patches of greens, his garden will have something growing in it the year round. His table will be loaded with wild fruits, such as blackberries, huckleberries, plums, etc. His potatoes will keep him from buying so much corn meal and flour on credit. He plans to raise more than enough corn, oats, and wheat to do him another year. Then he makes that cotton crop count. He gathers every lock of it as fast as it opens and tries to sell it for every cent it is worth. He walks up like a man and pays every cent he owes when it falls due. Then his neighbours, both white and coloured, learn to respect him because he is an honest man, he owes nobody, his store-house, smoke-house, and barn are loaded with fruits, and home-made produce. He is a happy man because that mortgage is lifted."

CHAPTER XII

I have always been intensely fond of outdoor life. Perhaps the explanation for this lies partly in the fact that I was born nearly out-of-doors. I have also, from my earliest childhood, been very fond of animals and fowls. When I was but a child, and a slave, I had many close and interesting acquaintances with animals.

During my childhood days, as a slave, I did not see very much of my mother, as she was obliged to leave her children very early in the morning to begin her day's work. Her early departure often made the matter of my securing breakfast uncertain. This led to my first intimate acquaintance with animals.

In those days it was the custom upon the plantation to boil the Indian corn that was fed to the cows and pigs. At times, when I had failed to get any other breakfast, I used to go to the places where the cows and pigs were fed, and share their breakfast with them, or else go to the place where it was the custom to boil the corn, and get my morning meal there before it was taken to the animals.

If I was not there at the exact moment of feeding, I could still find enough corn scattered around the fence or the trough to satisfy me. Some people may think that this was a pretty bad way to get one's food, but, leaving out the name and the associations, there was nothing very bad about it. Any one who has eaten hard boiled corn knows that it has a delicious taste. I never pass a pot of boiled corn now without yielding to the temptation to eat a few grains.

Another thing that assisted in developing my fondness for animals was my contact with the best breeds of fowls and animals when I was a student at the Hampton Institute. Notwithstanding that my work there was not directly connected with the stock, the mere fact that I saw the best kinds of animals and fowls day·after day increased my love for them, and made me resolve that when I went out into the world I would have some as nearly like those as possible.

I think that I owe a great deal of my present strength and capacity for hard work to my love of outdoor life. It is true that the amount of time that I can spend in the open air is now very limited. Taken on an average, it is perhaps not more than an hour a day, but I make the most of that hour. In addition to this, I get much pleasure out of looking forward to and planning for that hour.

I do not believe that any one who has not worked

in a garden can begin to understand how much pleasure and strength of body and mind and soul can be derived from one's garden, no matter how small it may be, and often the smaller it is the better. If the garden be ever so limited in area, one may still have the gratifying experience of learning how much can be produced on a little plot carefully laid out, thoroughly fertilised, and intelligently cultivated. And then, though the garden may be small, if the flowers and vegetables prosper, there springs up a feeling of kinship between the man and his plants, as he tends and watches the growth of each individual fruition from day to day. Every morning brings some fresh development, born of the rain, the dew, and the sunshine.

The letter or the address you began writing the day before never grows until you return and take up the work where it was left off; not so with the plant. Some change has taken place during the night, in the appearance of bud, or blossom, or fruit. This sense of newness, of expectancy, brings to me a daily inspiration whose sympathetic significance it is impossible to convey in words.

It is not only a pleasure to grow vegetables for one's table, but I find much satisfaction, also, in sending selections of the best specimens to some neighbour whose garden is backward, or to one who has not learned the art of raising the finest or the earliest varieties, and who is therefore surprised to receive new potatoes two weeks in advance of any one else.

When I am at my home in Tuskegee, I am able, by rising early in the morning, to spend at least half an hour in my garden, or with my fowls, pigs, or cows. Whenever I can take the time, I like to hunt for the new eggs each morning myself, and when at home I am selfish enough to permit no one else to make these discoveries. As with the growing plants, there is a sense of freshness and restfulness in the finding and handling of newly laid eggs that is delightful to me. Both the anticipation and the realisation are most pleasing. I begin the day by seeing how many eggs I can find, or how many little chickens are just beginning to peep through the shells.

Speaking of little chickens coming into life reminds me that one of our students called my attention to a fact connected with the chickens owned by the school which I had not previously known. When some of the first little chickens came out of their shells, they began almost immediately to help others, not so forward, to break their way out. It was delightful to me to hear that the chickens raised at the school had, so early in life, caught the Tuskegee spirit of helpfulness toward others.

I am deeply interested in the different kinds of fowls, and, aside from the large number grown by the school in its poultry house and yards, I grow at

When at Tuskegee I Find a Way by Rising Early in the Morning to Spend Half an Hour in My Garden or with the Live Stock

my own home common chickens, Plymouth Rocks, Buff Cochins, and Brahmas, Peking ducks, and fantailed pigeons.

The pig, I think, is my favourite animal. In addition to some common-bred pigs, I keep a few Berkshires and some Poland Chinas; and it is a pleasure to me to watch their development and increase from month to month. Practically all the pork used in my family is of my own raising.

I heard not long ago a story of one of our graduates which delighted me as an illustration of the real Tuskegee spirit. A man had occasion to go to the village of Benton, Alabama, in which Mr. A. J. Wood, one of our graduates, had settled ten years before, and gone into business as a general merchant. In this time he has built up a good trade and has obtained for himself a reputation as one of the best and most reliable business men in the place. While the visitor was there, he happened to step to the open back door of the store, and stood looking out into a little yard behind the building. The merchant joining him there, began to call, "Ho, Boy. Ho, Boy," and finally, in response to this calling, there came crawling out from beneath the store, with much grunting, because he was altogether too big to get comfortably from under the building, an enormous black hog.

"You see that hog," the man said. "That's my hog. I raise one like that every year as an object-lesson to the coloured farmers around here who come to the store to trade. About all I feed him is the waste from the store. When the farmers come in here, I show them my hog, and I tell them that if they would shut their pigs up in a pen of rails, and have the children pick up acorns in the woods to feed them on, they might have just such hogs as I do, instead of their razor-backs running around wild in the woods.

"Perhaps I can't teach a school here," the man added, "but if I can't do that, I can at least teach the men around here how to raise hogs as I learned to raise them at Tuskegee."

In securing the best breeds of fowls and animals at Tuskegee, I have the added satisfaction of seeing a better grade of stock being gradually introduced among the farmers who live near the school.

After I have gathered my eggs, and have at least said "Good morning" to my pigs, cows, and horse, the next morning duty—no, I will not say duty, but delight—is to gather the vegetables for the family dinner. No pease, no turnips, radishes nor salads taste so good as those which one has raised and gathered with his own hands in his own garden. In comparison with these all the high-sounding dishes found in the most expensive restaurants seem flavourless. One feels, when eating his own fresh vegetables, that he is getting near to the heart of nature; not a second-hand stale imitation,

HOGS AS OBJECT LESSONS

but the genuine thing. How delightful the change, after one has spent weeks eating in restaurants or hotels, and has had a bill of fare pushed before his eyes three times a day, or has heard the familiar sound for a month from a waiter's lips: "Steak, pork chops, fried eggs, and potatoes."

As I go from bed to bed in the garden, gathering my lettuce, pease, spinach, radishes, beets, onions and the relishes with which to garnish the dishes, and note the growth of each plant since the previous day, I feel a nearness and kinship to the plants which makes them seem to me like members of my own family. When engaged in this work, how short the half-hour is, how quickly each minute goes, bringing nearer the time when I must go to my office. When I do go there it is with a vigour and freshness and with a steadiness of nerve that prepares me thoroughly for what perhaps is to be a difficult and trying day—a preparation impossible, except for the half-hour spent in my garden.

All through the day I am enabled to do more work and better work because of the delightful anticipation of another half-hour or more in my garden after the office work is done. I get so much pleasure out of this that I frequently find myself beseeching Mrs. Washington to delay the dinner hour that I may take advantage of the last bit of daylight for my outdoor work.

My own experience in outdoor life leads me to

hope that the time will soon come when there will be a revolution in our methods of educating children, especially in the schools of the smaller towns and rural districts.   I consider it almost a sin to take a number of children whose homes are on farms, and whose parents earn their living by farming, and cage them up, as if they were so many wild beasts, for six or seven hours during the day, in a close room where the air is often impure.

I have known teachers to go so far as to frost the windows in a school-room, or have them made high up in the wall, or keep the window curtains down, so that the children could not even see the wonderful world without.   For six hours the life of these children is an artificial one.   The apparatus which they use is, as a rule, artificial, and they are taught in an artificial manner about artificial things. Even to whisper about the song of a mocking-bird or the chirp of a squirrel in a near-by tree, or to point to a stalk of corn or a wild flower, or to speak about a cow and her calf, or a little colt and its mother grazing in an adjoining field, are sins for which they must be speedily and often severely punished.   I have seen teachers keep children caged up on a beautiful, bright day in June, when all Nature was at her best, making them learn—or try to learn—a lesson about hills, or mountains, or lakes, or islands, by means of a map or globe, when the land surrounding the school-house was alive

and beautiful with the images of these things. I
have seen a teacher work for an hour with children,
trying to impress upon them the meaning of the
words lake, island, peninsula, when a brook not a
quarter of a mile away would have afforded the
little ones an opportunity to pull off their shoes and
stockings and wade through the water, and find, not
one artificial island or lake, on an artificial globe,
but dozens of real islands, peninsulas, and bays.
Besides the delight of wading through the water,
and of being out in the pure bracing air, they would
learn by this method more about these natural
divisions of the earth in five minutes than they
could learn in an hour in books. A reading lesson
taught out on the green grass under a spreading oak
tree is a lesson needing little effort to hold a boy's
attention, to say nothing of the sense of delight and
relief which comes to the teacher.

I have seen teachers compel students to puzzle
for hours over the problem of the working of the
pulley, when not a block from the school-house were
workmen with pulleys in actual operation, hoisting
bricks for the walls of a new building.

I believe that the time is not far distant when
every school in the rural districts and in the small
towns will be surrounded by a garden, and that
one of the objects of the course of study will be to
teach the child something about real country life,
and about country occupations.

I am glad to say that at the Tuskegee Institute we erected a school-house in and about which the little children of the town and vicinity are given a knowledge, not only of books, but of the real things which they will be called upon to use in their homes. Since Tuskegee is surrounded by people who earn their living by agriculture, we have near this school-house three acres of ground on which the children are taught to cultivate flowers, shrubbery, vegetables, grains, cotton, and other crops. They are also taught cooking, laundering, sewing, sweeping, and dusting, how to set a table, and how to make a bed—the employments of their daily lives. I have referred to this building as a "school-house," but we do not call it that, because the name is too formal. We have named it "The Children's House." And this principle holds true, for children of a larger growth, and is especially true of the training of the Negro minister who serves the people of the smaller towns and country districts.

In this, as in too many other educational fields, the Negro minister is trained to meet conditions which exist in New York or in Chicago—in a word, it is too often taken for granted that there is no difference between the work to be done by Negro ministers among our people after only thirty-five years of freedom, and that to be done among the white people who have had the advantages of centuries of freedom and development.

TEACH THE CHILD SOMETHING ABOUT REAL COUNTRY LIFE

The Negro ministers, except those sent to the large cities, go among an agricultural people, a people who lead an outdoor life. They are poor, without homes or ownership in farms, without proper knowledge of agriculture. They are able to pay their minister so small and uncertain a salary that he can not live on it honestly and pay his bills promptly.

During the three or four years that the minister has spent in the theological class room, scarcely a single subject that concerns the every-day life of his future people has been discussed. He is taught more about the soil of the valley of the Nile, or of the valley of the river Jordan, than about the soil of the State in which the people of his church are to live and to work.

What I urge is that the Negro minister should be taught something about the outdoor life of the people whom he is to lead. More than that, it would help the problem immensely if in some more practical and direct manner this minister could be taught to get the larger portion of his own living from the soil—to love outdoor work, and to make his garden, his farm, and his farm-house object-lessons for his people.

The Negro minister who earns a large part of his living on the farm is independent, and can reprove and rebuke the people when they do wrong. This is not true of him who is wholly dependent upon his congregation for his bread. What is equally important, an interest in agricultural production and a love for work tend to keep a minister from that idleness which may prove a source of temptation.

At least once a week, when I am in the South, I make it a practice to spend an hour or more among the people of Tuskegee and vicinity—among the merchants and farmers, white and black. In these talks with the real people I can get at the actual needs and conditions of those for whom our institution is at work.

When talking to a farmer, I feel that I am talking with a real man and not an artificial one— one who can keep me in close touch with the real things. From a simple, honest cultivator of the soil, I am sure of getting first-hand, original information. I have secured more useful illustrations for addresses in a half-hour's talk with some white or coloured farmer than from hours of reading books.

If I were a minister, I think I should make a point of spending a day in each week in close, unconventional touch with the masses of the people. A vacation employed in visiting farmers, it seems to me, would often prepare one as thoroughly for his winter's work as a vacation spent in visiting the cities of Europe.

CHAPTER XIII

On the Experimental Farm

THE purpose most eagerly sought by the Agricultural Department of the Tuskegee Institute is to demonstrate to the farmers of Alabama, first of all, that with right methods their acres can be made to yield unfailing profit, and that they can win in the fight against the deadly mortgage system. In many of the Western and Northwestern States cheese-making has led the one-crop, wheat-growing farmers to independence. The South has felt that this industry was beyond its reach, and has set small store by the dairy business. At Tuskegee, not only has it been demonstrated that cows can be made to yield from 50 to 150 per cent. on the money invested, but also that every farmer can, at moderate cost, make his own cheese, with a good supply for the market. Not long ago, the graduate of the Institute who is directly in charge of the cheese and butter departments, sent to my home specimens of six kinds of cheese made at the school —Tuskegee Cream, Philadelphia Cream Cheese, Neufchatel, Cottage, Club-house, and Cheddar. These were as fine grades of cheese as can be found in any other creamery.

To find out what corn, grasses, pease, millet, etc., are best suited to the Southern climate and soil is the work of several years of earnest labour. At present experiments are in progress with ten varieties of corn, with vetch, clovers, cassava, sugar beet, Cuban sugar cane, eight kinds of millet, the Persian and Arabian beans, and many other food and forage plants. Fifty-five acres of peach orchard are sowed in pease, besides three hundred acres of corn land utilised for this second or auxiliary crop. The vegetable garden covers fifty acres, and there is hardly a day when this garden fails to help pay the table expenses of the school.

Stock raising is carried on more extensively each year. To get the best hog, sheep, cow, and horse for this region of the country is the chief aim. We cannot quit cotton, but we must raise our stock and our meat. The hen and the bee are great wealth-producers, but not more than one in three hundred Macon County families raise bees, and few of them give any special care to poultry. Therefore the school trustees spend a large sum of money each year in teaching the practical lessons of these industries.

Statistical data show that the average yield of cotton per acre throughout the South is 190 pounds, an astonishingly low figure, and, except when high prices rule, below the paying point. Every acre of cotton in the South can and should be made to

CULTIVATING A PATCH OF CASSAVA ON THE AGRICULTURAL EXPERIMENT PLOT

produce 500 pounds of lint. Should the cotton grower add the trifling increase of five pounds of lint an acre, it would mean for the Cotton States a total increase of 240,000 bales, based on the crop reports for 1902, with a value of nearly $15,000,000, according to the prices realised on the crop of 1903. The experimental station at Tuskegee has appreciated the tremendous possibilities pictured by such statements as these, and the Director, Mr. Carver, has demonstrated the value of scientific cultivation, by raising nearly 500 pounds of cotton on one acre of poor Alabama land. In addition he has taken up the problem of crossing varieties of cotton to increase the quality of the uplands staple. These experiments have been promisingly successful, and already a hybrid cotton has been grown which is vastly superior to that commonly raised in Alabama. In other words, Tuskegee is teaching the farmers how to raise a better grade of cotton and more of it, without increasing the acreage planted.

The subject of soil improvement through natural agencies has been one of much concern to both ancient and modern agriculturists. The ancient Egyptian knew that if he let his land lie idle—"rested," as he termed it—he was able to produce a much better crop, and that crop would be in quantity and quality, all other things being equal, proportionate to the length of time this land had been rested.

At a later period the fertilising value of the legumes (pod-bearing plants) was recognised. But as the population of the world increased and civilisation advanced, it became more imperative that all farming operations should be more intensive and less extensive. Each decade saw the progressive farmer on his journey of progress correcting many mistakes of the past. He then began to see that it was quite possible and practicable to keep his ground covered with some crop; and the soil also became richer and more fertile every year—by reason of this constant tillage—than was possible under the old method of letting the land lie fallow for a few years. As science shed light upon his art, he learned that the crop-yielding capacity of a soil was increased by rotating or changing his farm crops every year upon land not occupied by such crops the year previous.

For seven years Tuskegee has made the subject of crop rotation a special study, and submits the plan illustrated by the accompanying chart as the most simple and satisfactory. This chart and data were worked out by the Director of the Agricultural Department. It was hoped that the experiment would shed some light on the following pertinent questions:

(a) Is it possible to build up the poor upland soils of Alabama?

(b) Can injurious washing away of the soil by rains be overcome?

(c) Are not the fertilisers necessary for the production of a crop on such land far beyond the reach of the average farmer?

(d) Granting it can be built up and made productive, will it not take an average life-time?

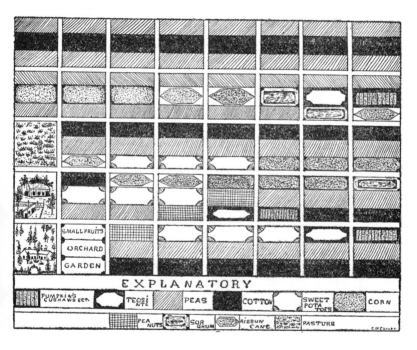

(e) Will it pay to purchase such land?

(f) State the smallest amount of such land the farmer should buy expecting to make a living off it.

The plan for rotation as outlined is for a farm of **forty acres**, but is perfectly applicable to one of any size, even down to a garden patch. In order that our efforts might be guided with the greatest degree of intelligence, the soil was analysed and found to be seriously deficient in three very important elements of plant food, and in the order named: Nitrogen, phosphoric acid and potash. In addition to this, it was practically devoid of humus (vegetable matter), and otherwise was in as bad a physical condition as chemical. Our first efforts were directed toward correcting the physical condition by deep plowing, rebuilding terraces and filling in washes. This being done, we are now ready to make definite plans for planting our forty-acre farm. In a farm this size we find it is wise to set aside four acres to be used as indicated:

(1) One acre for the house, lawn, flower garden, nut and ornamental trees. (2) One acre for the garden, orchard and small fruits. Upon this all the vegetables of various kinds, peaches, pears, plums, figs, strawberries, blackberries, grapes, etc., should be raised, not simply to supply the needs of the family, but there should be a surplus to market. (3) One acre for the barn, poultry house, pigsties, and other necessary out-buildings. (4) One acre for a good pasture where cows, horses, hogs, and stock of various kinds might be turned in from time to time. The remaining thirty-six acres should be planted as follows:

First year, sixteen acres of cowpease, eight acres

of cotton, two acres of ribbon cane, three acres of corn, one acre of sorghum, one acre of peanuts, three acres of sweet potatoes, one acre of teosinte (a green fodder plant), one acre of pumpkins, cushaws, squash, etc.

The second year it will be observed that the peas change places with the cotton, corn, ribbon cane, sorghum, teosinte, pumpkins and sweet potatoes, except in a few instances—and these are where the soil was: (a) Naturally poor, as indicated by the acre where peanuts and cowpease follow each other the first and second years in order to better fit the land physically and chemically to produce an exhaustive crop like cotton; (b) Sweet potatoes following cotton and ribbon cane. Here bottom land is represented, and is, therefore, quite fertile. The fertilisers necessary to produce a good crop of sugar cane and cotton were quite sufficient to produce a good crop of potatoes with but little additional fertiliser. (c) In this we have a different condition—that of neglected bottom soil, deficient mainly in nitrogen. Here the pea is planted the first year to restore the nitrogen; and this is followed by teosinte and sorghum in one instance and pumpkins and ribbon cane in another; the physical condition of the soil being best suited to these particular crops. With the few exceptions mentioned, the third year is identical with the first.

Such a system of rotation has enabled us in seven

*years to make a net profit of $96.22 from one acre of
this land, when in the beginning we lost $2.40 per acre.*

In 1897, cowpease were planted, using $5 worth of
kainite and acid phosphate per acre—mixing them
together and putting in the drill.   The seed, preparation of the land, planting, harvesting the light
crop of vines, etc., amounted to $6.50, making a
total of $11.50.   The crop sold for $9.10, leaving us
$2.40 behind.

In 1898, this same acre was planted in sweet
potatoes and fertilised with $5 worth of kainite and
acid phosphate, the same as recommended for the
pease.   The after-operation cost $6.   Fifty-five
bushels of marketable potatoes were harvested and
sold for 60c per bushel, equalling $33, and leaving a
net balance of $22 on the acre.

In 1899, cowpease were again planted and fertilised
exactly the same as in 1897.   The returns were
fifteen bushels of pease, at 55 cents per bushel, equalling $8.25 ; also one and one-half tons of cured hay,
worth $22.50, giving a total of $30.75.   Less the
cost—$11.50—equals $19.25 gain.

In 1900, it was planted in sorghum cane, fertilised
with $5 worth of kainite and acid phosphate, plus
fifteen one-horse wagon-loads of swamp muck and
decayed forest leaves, at a cost of $3.75 ; plus the
cost of harvesting, etc., $4.25, making a total of $13.
Seven tons of hay were harvested and sold green for
$5 a ton, leaving a gain of $22.

In 1901, cowpease were planted and fertilised exactly the same as for the sorghum.   Twenty-five bushels of pease were harvested, worth $13.75; two tons of cured hay worth $28, making a total of $41.75; less the cost, equals $28.75 gain.

In 1902, it was planted in garden truck—cabbage, onions, beets, squash, tomatoes, melons, beans, turnips, mustard, kale, kohl rabi, rutabagas, etc. Fertilised the same as for sorghum and pease, except half of the swamp muck was replaced by stable manure.   The total operations cost $21; the entire crop sold for $60, leaving a gain of $39.

In 1903, it was again planted in cowpease.   Fertilised the same as for the garden.   Twenty-seven bushels of pease were harvested, worth $14.85, and three tons of cured hay worth $43, equalling $56.85. Less the cost, gives us a gain of $43.85 per acre.

In this same year, a portion of this field, subject to the same rotation, was planted in white potatoes, using the same amount of muck, kainite and phosphate, at a total cost of $9.   Eighty bushels of potatoes were harvested and sold for $1 per bushel, equalling $80.   Before the potatoes were dug, cowpease were planted between the rows and yielded $25.22 worth of peas and hay, giving a clear profit of $96.22 per acre.

Another acre subjected to the same treatment was planted in early corn and followed by sweet potatoes, at a cost of $16.   It gave a crop as follows: $44.60

in corn and fodder, one hundred and five bushels of marketable potatoes, and $4.05 worth of hay; making in all $111.65. Less $16.90, gives a profit of $94.75.

It is important to note that the data for 1903 represent only one-half of the crop, as the land is now in grain and will be harvested in time for the next crop, or grazed, which, of course, will give a net balance according to the yield of this grain or its value in grazing. We think, therefore, that the foregoing facts answer quite conclusively all the questions in the affirmative, and that it is wise for the Southern farmer to purchase a home even of two acres.

CHAPTER XIV

The Eagerness for Learning

Necessity compels most of the coloured youth seeking education to work with their hands and pay as they go. It is better thus, even for those who do not expect to follow trades. I do not believe that any young man who has worked his way through Yale or Harvard regrets the experience. All whom I have met were proud of the achievement, and considered it an important part of the training that was to make them useful and capable men.

Many thousand letters of application for admission to the Tuskegee Institute are on file in my office. Their general trend is one of the strongest arguments for the gospel of hard work with head and hands. These young men and women from nearly every state of the Union and many foreign countries are writing me scores of letters daily, asking for a chance to get an education. With them there is no such thing as taking it for granted that they will be sent to school by somebody else. They have felt the force of newly awakened ambition, and lacking money to support themselves for three, four or five years in school, are eager to work for it. If their parents share this ambition, it is often the case that prayers, and heartfelt wishes, and hopes are all they can give their children to help them along the rough road to freedom.

For lack of room, we are forced to refuse each year thousands of applicants, earnest, pleading candidates, most of them, who are willing to make any sacrifices, to endure any burden of toil, to get the training that is to help them and enable them to help others. Merely to look through these piles of letters as they have accumulated for years would require many days' labour. I have chosen a few of them at random, for they show why Tuskegee students are in earnest from the beginning of their school work to the end, and why they go out to earn a living, armed with sincerity of purpose.

I have taken the liberty of making them easier to read by correcting the crude spelling and expression in some of them.

Here is one in which the writer has a fondness for imposing words without quite knowing how to handle them:

Dear President: I that delights in education have by recommendation conceived an idea of applying to your worthy school, if possible, for education, provided I am qualified to enter. Believing that your catalogue will give me a thorough understanding of the same, I will hereby [ask] that you send me one of your complete catalogues that I may prepare to enter the ensueing fall. Now, sir, you will please excuse me if I give you knowledge of my disposition. I am full of delight in education. Therefore I will try to be one of the most pious students of the time. This would also cause me to be grateful for the privileges, especially those of labour, for this is my first inquiry whether I might remain in school during vacation and work. In fact, I would have, please, sir, a prompt and continual job in school. Please, sir, to interest yourself in my welfare in this circumstance.

Dear Sir: Wishing to enter the Tuskegee Institute, I hereby write you for information. I wish to enter night school and work in the day as an apprentice in the machine department. My parents are poor and not able so assist me in going to school, so my only chance is to work my way if there be any chance at all. I am now twenty-one years old. I am working with my father on a farm where I have been working ever since I have been large enough. I have been going so school some, but a very little, while I were very small, and I had not been in several years until this Mr. —— came here, and now I am working every day and going to school at night. I am proud to say that he has done me good two ways by telling me of the chances afforded in the Tuskegee Institute for poor boys and girls to educate themselves, and he has enthused my ambition for educating and bettering my condition. Please send me a catalogue of the school, that I may see just how I must start to enter.
Yours truly, desiring an education.

Dear Sir: I have heard so much and read so much of your school, until I am craving to come and take a part with the leading people of my colour. Mr. Washington, I've heard that a poor person who desires to make a mark in the world and haven't the means, you would take them and let them work the first year for two hours lessons at night, and let this help on their expenses for the next year. If this is correct, will you please write me at once, for I am a poor girl, and is so very anxious to learn some good trade, also have good learning in books, and I am too poor to go to school and pay. So if you will let me in, I am willing to work very hard, indeed I am. Please send me a clear understanding of the school, for I am anxious to be a great woman. Please write me at an early date.

Dear Sir: I have read and heard a great deal of your school, and I want to attend it this summer. I would like to know whether I could work all of my way or not, as my parents is not able to send me, and I want to go to school, I want to take a special course in sewing.

Kind Sir: I received your immediate reply, and I was truly glad to hear from you, and to receive your circular of information and its meanings. But there is a few questions of importance I wish to ask. Can I enter the night school at once, or is there any limited time the school closes, and when are the sessions? Now, I hope I can enter at once, and stay the year around, or as long as I can be employed at the place, so that I can pay my board and schooling, as I have no parents and I am trying to make a start for an education. I am a member of the church and a lover of the Sunday School, also I feel that I have a superior calling from on high. Therefore I wish to secure even a good English education. May God provide for your success is the prayer of your humble servant.

Kind Sir: I have thought to write you since your lecture up here in the adjoining county last fall. Mr. Washington, I have a great desire for an education and it seems that I have many besetments in life that prohibits me from saving just the amount of money that I need to educate myself as I desire so do, and I will inquire of you if your college has any way that a young man could work his tuition out. If so, please let me know just what terms I could enter on, as I have fully made up my mind to try to educate myself, provided any school will help me in my struggle. I see the need of an education, and I see that there is fields of work for a young man of my age. Mr. Washington, if you please, give me a chance if you can, I am willing to work my way through at any position you would put me at to pay for my learning. I am not too proud to do any work I can help to educate myself. I want to join that goodly number of Negroes that is making such success at your school. Please pardon such a long letter   Your humble questioner.

Mr. Washington: I would be more than glad to appreciate your school, inasmuch as to come down and attend about two terms, if you are not filled. I am not able to pay my board in money, and if there is any vacancy in your school where I can

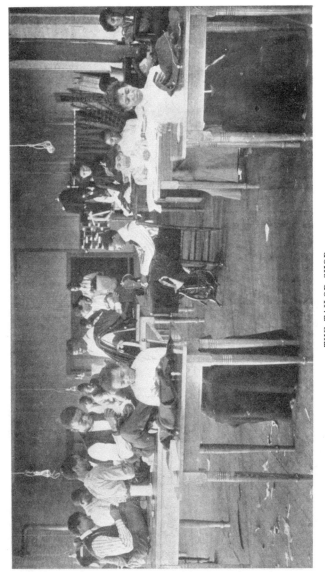

THE TAILOR SHOP

work and pay, I would be more than glad. Please let me know immediately, so I will know what to do. Let me know all about your charges per month. Please reply at once, because I want to come as early as possible.

Dear Sir: I received your kind circulars some days ago, and I was more than glad to hear as I did. I would have wrote before now, but thinking I could come soon, I waited. Though times is so hard, of course a poor boy that has no one to help him has a hard time, but by the help of the Lord, I am going to make a man of myself. I want to come as soon as I can. I am going to bring every one that will come with me. I want to stay there and work until I can master a trade.

Dear Sir: I takes great pleasure in writing to you a few lines, and hopes this will find you well. I want to complete the full course of education, and am not exactly able to bear my expenses through. I would like to know whether you will give me a position to work to pay my expenses through. If you will, it will be a great favour and consolation to me. Write soon, and let me hear from you, and please send me full particulars.

Dear Sir: After reading and hearing so much talk of your school, I made it up in my mind that I would like to attend your school, as I have been trying to get an education for the last two years. I attended school here in Texas for six months this term, but owing to my money running short I had to quit school and go to work. I am a poor boy, and I desire to get an education. Do you think that you could give me work to pay my school? I want an industrial education, and am not able to pay for it, and I will do any work I can get to pay for my lesson.

"I would like to attend your school, but being poor I can't enter as a day student. I write to know if I can enter as a work student. I would like to enter soon enough so that I can work during the summer months. Mr. Washington, I am anxious to get a good training. Being poor and fatherless, I have had few advantages, and that is why I have applied to you as I have. If you will or will not receive me, please let me know as soon as possible."

"I received your circular and was carefully reading the terms. There is some few more hints I would like to ask you. If I arrive there with forty dollars, could I attend the whole nine months of a school year? My occupation has been for the last four years cooking. Before then it was farming, but I can do a little laundry work also. In these four years I have attended school two terms in public school. I am very anxious for an industrial education, so therefore I desire to attend your school. The industrial studies I would like to learn are carriage-trimming and laundry work. My studies are United States History, Arithmetic, English, and Geography. If you think I can stay the whole term on forty dollars let me know, and I will be there in August. I am twenty-two years of age."

"Please let me know whether you can furnish girls work enough to support them in school. I see in the 'Voice of Missions' where you will give ministers work to support themselves. Is there any chance for a girl who wants an education? I have read of your school, and would like so well to come there, but I live so far away, until I would not be able to pay my fare from New Orleans and then pay my school expenses. Please let me know the cheapest that I could enter school, also the distance and cost from New Orleans. I would like to enter next season without fail. Please write me by return mail without fail."

Dear Sir: During your recent lecturing tour you stopped here and I was determined to hear you, and when I heard you I was fired with the ambition to go to school. I tried to get an audience with you, but owing to so many others who were as enthusiastic as I, I could only speak a few words with you. Do you remember the young man who spoke to you about going to your school? As I said before, I did not have time to explain it all to you. I am unable to pay my way through your school, but I am more than willing to work my way through. You told me that I could when I spoke to you about it.

Dear Sir: My boy ran away from home during my absence from home in January. After he was gone, I learned from his associates that he said he was going to Tuskegee to school. Please inform me whether he has made his appearance there or not.

Dear Sir: Do you think it best for me to enter as soon as possible, or wait until the next term, but I would rather enter as soon as possible. But will do as you think best. I have a mother and grandmother to support, and if I can get an education I know that I will be better fitted to support them, and I am sure that you will agree with me in the matter. And if you will give me a chance, I will be a man among my people some day.

Dear Sir: I am sorry that I cannot be admitted. In case of a vacancy, will you notify me, or until there is a chance could I come to the school in the summer? I am a poor girl. If I can't come in the summer, I am going to try to earn enough money to come and stay two or three months as soon as you will let me, even if there is no room to live at the school.

"I will write you a few lines to ask if you please to let me enter into your band of coloured scholars. That is, I want to come to your school in the daytime, or at night and work the rest of the time. If there is any way fixed, let me know whether my name can be put in your roll book. I have just left school a few days ago, and I want to get in as soon as possible. I have been striving to come to your school going on three years, and at last I have got to the point that if you will let me in I will be over there the first day of March. Please, sir, let me in, if there is any way that can be fixed to do so. I would be one of the happiest boys in the world if you say I could come. Please write me word just as soon as you read it."

Dear Sir: Having just read again a short biography of your life, and being desirous of obtaining a better education, I thought I would write you and perhaps gain the necessary information. Last year I completed the course in the High School here. When school opened in September, I joined the Normal Training Class here and since then I have been training in for a second and third grade teacher. I have had about eight months of piano music and two of vocal, and one school year in the elements of elocution. I am desirous of becoming a school teacher, and realise how necessary it is to have a better education. I have no support but an aged mother. I had almost given up hope, but when I read of others working their way through college, I am resolved to try. Is there any possible way of earning my schooling at Tuskegee? I thought perhaps I could teach in the primary grades a part of the day to pay for what I should get. Or perhaps I could work in some other way. I am willing to do any honest labour to get an education. You doubtless get letters of this kind daily, but I only ask that you please answer and tell me if there is any chance for a poor girl obtaining knowledge. I am so anxious that I would willingly work during the vacations and holidays. Please answer this, and if I cannot gain entrance at Tuskegee, perhaps you can tell me of some school where I can. If your answer is favorable, I will immediately begin to earn money to pay my way there, for those of us who are in the training class receive no salary.

CHAPTER XV

THE VALUE OF SMALL THINGS

A LIFETIME of hard work has shown me the value of little things of every day. We preach them at Tuskegee, and try to enforce them in the daily round of sixteen hundred students' lives. We speak of them because they are at the bottom of character-building, and because no person can go on year by year forgetting them, without having his soul warped and made small and weak. We want young men and women to go out, not as slaves of their daily routine, but masters of their circumstances. But the structure must be built a brick at a time, and no act is without its influence. I am in the habit of talking to the student body when it is assembled in the chapel for the first time after the opening of the school year with a good deal of practical exhortation about the "value of little things," unimportant as some of them may seem to the new-comers at Tuskegee. They are told, for example, that among the resolutions which each should abide by through the term, is to keep in close and constant touch with their homes. "You can do this," I have said, "in no better way than by forming the habit of writing a letter home once every week. I fear that this is not always done. I want to see each one of you grow into the habit of writing a letter to your parents or your friends at home, as often as you can find the time. I do not mean by this that you shall get a little piece of waste paper, snatch up a lead pencil, and scribble a hasty note, asking them to send you some money, or to send you a dress, or a hat. I mean for you to select a time—the Sabbath, if you can find no other time—and sit down in your rooms, or go to the library, take plenty of time, get good paper, the best ink, and write your mother and father, your brothers and sisters, a good, encouraging, well-thought-out letter. It will pay you to do that, even if you look at it from a selfish standpoint. Grow into the habit of doing that every week while you are students here.

"It will keep you in touch with your homes, and it always pays to keep under the home influence, no matter how humble that home may be, no matter how much poverty there may be about it, no matter how much ignorance there may be in it—it always pays to keep in close touch with your homes. I want you to do this, not only for your own sake, but more for the sake of your parents, for the sake of those who are trying to keep you at this institution. You can make them feel your appreciation in no better way than by writing them regularly in the manner that I have tried to urge you to do. It will encourage them. It will make them feel that it pays to make the sacrifice for you."

These practical talks on the value of small things are enforced by a corp of inspectors, whose practised eyes are quick to detect the soiled collar, the loose button, the unpolished boot, when the forces assemble for meals and for chapel, and the personal appearance of every student is carefully scrutinised. Nothing is more humiliating to a Tuskegee boy or girl than to be taken out of line as the body marches out of chapel.

It requires care and thought to make a hasty toilet after a ten-hour day on the farm or in the shops, and be ready for supper on the stroke of the bell. And a student late to meals goes without that meal unless he has a good excuse. But out of such a system arises a pride in personal appearance, and a spirit of self-respect that goes far toward making useful men and women. It must be remembered, too, that much of the raw material which is taken in hand at Tuskegee has not had the advantages of any system and order at home, even in the primary qualities of personal cleanliness and neatness.

It sounds like the discipline of a man-of-war to say that one loose or missing button on the clothing of any one of a thousand boys is almost instantly noted and recorded, but the students themselves are proud of the fact that it is seldom that one of them

must be called out of line by an inspector. They
have responded to the test set for them, and they
never forget it. They feel a personal sorrow that
the epithet "shiftless" has been used to characterise
their race, and they realise that it must be lived
down in small things as well as great.

There is a student police force at Tuskegee, the
members of which are uniformed and allowed to
carry policemen's short "clubs" on their night
rounds. A visitor, who was on his way to my house,
to dine, met at the gate a young man in uniform,
apparently on guard, who saluted with his raised
stick. My guest expressed some surprise, saying:

"I did not know that you had to guard against the
hostility of the Southern white people of this region.
It is shocking to know that race antagonism can be
so violent and unreasonable."

I replied: "I have no better friends than the
white people of Tuskegee, and there is no need for
a body guard, I assure you. That alarming young
man was simply a student policeman who saluted
you as he is required to do all teachers and visitors.
He is allowed to carry a stick, not because he will
ever need to use it, but because it is a badge of his
authority, an emblem of the responsibility of his
position. The officers of our cadet corps carry
swords for the same reasons."

The boy policeman and his club typify the worth
of little things, indirectly furnishing a help toward

the complex structure of character. The young man in uniform, trudging on his night rounds about the school grounds, feels himself more of a man if he is equipped for a man's work. It adds to his self-respect, and it helps him to feel that his duty is an important one.

The Savings Bank Department of the school, which is part of the regularly authorised banking department of the institution, has been, in addition to its education in business methods, a great aid in teaching the students the value of little things. Early in the present year, there were to the credit of the students in the savings fund deposits of more than $14,000. This was largely made up of small accounts. The depositors are allowed to have check-books, and to draw on their accounts checks in as small amounts as twenty-five cents. As a result they do not carry their available cash around in their pockets, but hasten to the bank with it, and settle nearly all transactions among themselves by check.

This impresses on their minds the value of saving, for the bank account is in itself a strong incentive. These deposits come from various sources. The work done by the students in the various industrial departments is not paid for in cash, but its value is credited to their accounts with the school for the board, lodging, laundry, etc., furnished them. Their work amounted last year to a cash value of more than $90,000.

For "ready money," however, they must depend on what they receive from home, which is a small proportion of the total bank deposits, and upon what they are able to earn out of working hours. Many of them act as agents on commission for mail-order houses, which supply clothing, shoes, underwear, and a variety of necessaries and a few luxuries. In the summer a large number of young men go from Tuskegee to work in the Southern States, many of them in the Alabama coal fields, to earn money to pay the expenses of their education through the next school year. They save these earnings and bring them back to deposit in the Institute bank.

But these savings are not in dollars for the most part, but in quarters, dimes, and even pennies. In looking over the books of the bank recently, the individual ledger accounts attracted my notice. There was a whole page given the account of one girl, whose individual deposits did not average more than ten cents. There were several of three cents, and one of two cents. It seemed to me that this girl student was worth watching in after life. If she was willing to walk across the grounds and back, a round trip of perhaps half a mile, from her dormitory or work-shop, to make a deposit of three cents in the savings bank, and to continue her deposits, although she was never able to save more than a few cents at a time, she was fast learning the value of small things, and was already far along the path of practical usefulness.

One thousand students assemble three times a day in the main dining-hall. They take their seats without confusion or noise. A line of young men and women face each other at each table, and over them presides a student host and a hostess. The young women are seated first, and then the young men march in. But no conversation is allowed until all are seated, and until after a simple grace is chanted by this chorus of a thousand voices.

The meal is something more than a necessary consumption of food. The deference which a young man should always pay to woman is taught, without demonstration, by the manner of assembling. Self-restraint is taught the girls by waiting five minutes in their seats before they begin to eat and to talk. Their meeting at table inculcates good manners. The boys are on their mettle to act like gentlemen, and the host and hostess feel a personal responsibility for enforcing the little details of courtesy and good breeding.

The corps of teachers assembles for meals in another dining-room. They are not needed to preserve order or enforce discipline, as the students have that matter largely in their own hands. Inspectors see that their clothes have been brushed, their faces and hands cleaned of the stains of the farm and work shops, as the army enters the dining-

hall.   But behaviour takes care of itself.   It is not
long since I read of riotous scenes in the "commons"
of certain Northern universities, in which students
were guilty of throwing bread and crockery around
the room.   This has never happened at Tuskegee,
and this kind of disorder in our dining-hall is quite
beyond my imagination.

Once in a while, when tired of office work, I walk
across the school grounds and drop into one of the
dormitories to talk with the boys or girls in their
rooms, and see for myself how they are living and
what they are doing to make their rooms, not only
spotlessly neat, but livable and attractive.   Not
long ago I went into a room in one of the girls' halls,
which was clean but utterly cheerless.   She said in
explanation that she had been told that, if she
could not keep the photographs and all the other
bric-a-brac that finds its way into a girl's room
dustless and in order, she should store the superfluous
articles away.   I told her that the result of this
misguided endeavour was a room that looked as much
like a barn as it did a home.   She told me how much
she had spent during the term in buying chocolate
to make "fudge."   For the same outlay she could
have had pretty framed prints on her walls, and
other simple adornment in good taste and without
"clutter."   That evening I said, while talking to
the students in chapel:

"I was in the rooms of several girls to-day.   I

had been in these rooms before. Some of the rooms are always clean and attractive. You will find a number of little, delicate, home-like touches about them. You have only to go into another room, and you will feel as if you wanted to go out as soon as possible. This latter room has possibly two or three girls in it, and they are always full of excuses, always explaining. They can stand for five, ten, fifteen minutes, and reel off excuses by the yard. Those girls, unless they change, will never get ahead very far, I fear.

"The habit of making excuses, of giving explanations, instead of achieving results, grows from year to year upon one, until finally it gets such a hold that I think the victim finds himself almost as well satisfied with a good, long-drawn-out excuse, as he does with real tangible achievement. The school-boy and girl must be taught such lessons in every moment of routine duty, and there are no "little things," to be carelessly overlooked, without danger that repetition will breed bad habit. The student may think these things are little, but permanent injury to character is the price paid for indifference and carelessness. The price is paid in permanent injury to character.

"Every dollar received at Tuskegee comes through hard work on the part of some one. Every dollar is placed with us because the donor feels that perhaps it will accomplish more good here than elsewhere.

It is always a question for them to choose between giving a dollar here or to some other institution. The attitude of every student, if he wishes to be honest, must be that he has no right to ask persons to support the school if a dollar goes into the hands of an individual who is not doing his very best to earn the worth of it, every moment of every day, from rising bell to "taps" on the bugle at the boy's hall."

Looking at education from this view-point, every detail of the work and administration of a community of sixteen hundred people, with their great variety of activities, becomes vitally important, a part toward the complete whole.

This doctrine of "small things" finds expression in an infinite number of channels. One of the despised but abundant products of the Southern farms has been the cowpea. It is used extensively as a fodder plant, and as a fertiliser by plowing it under. The cowpea is also one of the most nutritious of foods, when properly cooked, but while it has been growing at their doors the coloured people have neglected it as a part of their diet. The Tuskegee agricultural expert investigated the cowpea. He found that it was as valuable for food as the far-famed "Boston bean," and prepared his table of analyses to prove it. Then he worked out no less than eighteen different appetising recipes for cooking the humble cowpea, and made practical

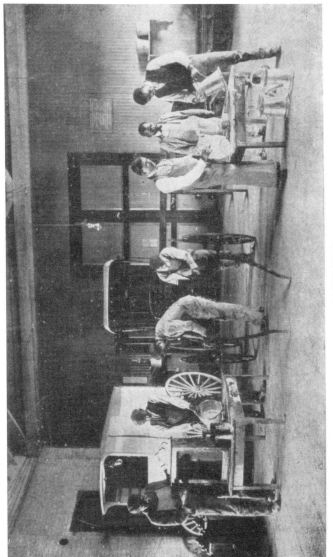

THE PAINT SHOP

demonstration, in a booth of his own making, during one of the Negro Conference gatherings.

These recipes he had printed for distribution in a neat and attractive pamphlet, and in this way he opened in defense of the cowpea a successful crusade, which has had direct results. It was a small thing, but it was not too small to be overlooked in the effort to make the best of the resources close at hand.

CHAPTER XVI

Religious Influences at Tuskegee

In the rapid growth of the institution along academic and industrial lines, the spiritual side of the school has not been neglected. During the last fifteen years a regularly appointed chaplain, an ordained evangelical minister, has been connected with the school, which is non-denominational, but by no means non-religious. It has much of the machinery of most regularly organised churches, although, for good reasons, it has not seemed best, yet, to organise a church in connection with the institution. It has, in fact, a much better equipment than most churches about it, both as to its house of worship and auxiliary services.

First: There is, each Sunday, a regular preaching service, at which teachers and students are expected to be present.

Second: Every Sunday morning, during the months of school, a large and enthusiastic Christian Endeavour Society meets for an hour's appropriate exercises. Teachers and students alike belong to it, serve on its committees, and, in many ways, are very helpful to the religious side of the school. The selections of scripture read or repeated and commented upon, the prayers offered, and the songs contributed by the students, show that they are preparing themselves for leadership in religion as well as for usefulness in shop and class room when they leave Tuskegee.

Third: The students are divided into thirty-six Sunday-school classes, each Sunday, to study the international lesson. There is also a Junior Sunday-school, composed of the children of teachers and of families near the school.

Fourth: A flourishing organisation of the Y. M. C. A., ably officered by students, makes itself felt for good both among the young men students as well as by visits, through committees, to the surrounding country, each Sunday, to look after sick and needy persons, especially the aged poor.

Fifth: The young women students, under the leadership of lady teachers, sustain three societies among themselves, viz.: The One Cent Missionary Society, the oldest in the institution. It is auxiliary to the Woman's Home Missionary Association of Boston, to which it sends $5 annually. The Edna D. Chaney Missionary Club has its own special work, as has also the Y. W. C. T. U. Recently, there has been organised a Y. W. C. A. to reach a younger class of girls. Each of these organisations has proved itself a potent factor for good, not only in the school and its immediate environs, but beyond; for it is the policy of the Tuskegee Institute to spread its various influences to other towns and communities, wherever its graduates and students find work, in whatever capacity.

Sixth: The Humane Society has done much to teach the students the proper care of dumb animals.

Seventh: The Tuskegee Women's Club, a branch of the National Association of Coloured Women, which meets twice a month to discuss such topics as look to the betterment of the women and girls of the Negro race in the United States. Another society, more local, is called Mothers' Council. Here the married women meet to discuss household matters. One of the members of this body, the wife of an instructor, though herself not a teacher, has for several years been conducting a Sunday afternoon meeting for neglected children in one of the tenement sections of the town of Tuskegee. The room in which the meetings are held is rented for this purpose by the students of the Bible School and paid for out of their weekly contributions.

Eighth: Once, daily, at evening (Friday and Saturday excepted), the whole school assembles in the spacious chapel for devotional services, led by the Principal or his representative, before retiring.

Ninth: Perhaps the most helpful religious meeting of all is the Friday evening prayer-meeting, where teachers and students gather, before retiring, as one large family, for informal worship; for it is the most home-like of all the services. Any one is at liberty to take part, without restraint, and at times so much interest is manifested that it often happens that two or more will be on their feet at the same time striving to get a hearing, or will raise hymns or begin to pray, or speak or repeat verses of Scripture at the same time. But the utmost courtesy and good nature prevail. These meetings are productive of much good. Many of the students date their conversion from the impulse received at these Friday evening meetings.

Tenth: The Week of Prayer is usually observed for two weeks, in January, every year, with more or less spiritual profit to the whole institution. The outward results from the meetings held during the present year are the hopeful and happy conversions of more than one hundred and fifty students, from all classes, post-graduates, special students, down through the preparatory grades. The most of these have received, and, after careful and prayerful consideration, have signed, in duplicate, the following pledge, keeping one copy and returning the other to the Chaplain:

MY PLEDGE.

I thank God that I was led by the Spirit to accept Christ. I am glad I am a Christian, and I promise:

1. That, as soon as I can, I will join the church of my choice, and by word and deed help to build up the kingdom of Christ on earth.

2. That I will, daily, think of, or read some portion of the

Bible, and will pray, in private each day of my life, closing each prayer with this verse:

> "Lord Jesus, I long to be perfectly whole;
> I want Thee forever to live in my soul;
> Break down every idol, cast out every foe:
> Now wash me and I shall be whiter than snow."
>
> —Amen.

Name ....

P. O. address.......................................

....

The reclamation of many backsliders also, as well as the spiritual awakening of the teacher's, many of whom joined heartily in the work of soul-saving, were gratifying and encouraging results.

Eleventh: Last, but not least, is the wholesome influence the Bible Training School has on the entire Institute.

This school is a department of the Normal and Industrial Institute. It was founded some years ago by a lady living in New York, in order that poor young men and women might be enabled, on the Tuskegee plan, to fit themselves for the Christian ministry and other active religious work.

A night class is connected with the Bible School, to reach those who cannot attend during the day, but who are desirous of knowing more about the Bible. The members of this class are the farmers and other labouring men who live in the neighbourhood. They come twice a week for an hour and a half, some of them walking two, three, four, and five miles each way, and show the greatest interest in the lessons. Most of them are pastors and members of churches in their communities. The students of the Bible School are expected to spend their Sundays in religious work among the churches and mission stations in the surrounding country. Every Sunday morning they may be seen, in groups of two or more, starting out, after breakfast, to their various appointments, reaching from four to six miles into the country, and to the jail and the churches in the town of Tuskegee. If they do not find a place of labour, they are encouraged to begin in new fields, and to reach people who might otherwise be neglected. Several have started missions, and two, during the history of the Bible School, have organised and built churches, and turned them over to their respective denominational connections. The Bible students are required to make a weekly report of their outside work on the following blank:

WEEKLY REPORT
OF THE
RELIGIOUS WORK DONE IN TUSKEGEE AND VICINITY,
BY STUDENTS OF
PHELPS HALL BIBLE TRAINING SCHOOL

Work done for the week ending Sunday night........19
1. Name of student.................Are you a minister
   Licentiate or a Layman?.........................
2. What is your denomination?........................

3. Where do you labour?..............(State whether in a church, jail, or almshouse, etc.)....................

4. Sermons, Give:

       1st. Number preached.........................

       2nd. Scriptures read..........................

       3d. The text to each.........................

       4th. The subjects to each......................

5. Number of adults present?...........................

       1st. Males.......................................

       2nd. Females..................................

       3rd. Children..................................

6. Number of Sunday Schools attended?..................

       Number of children present...................

       1st. Males......................................

       2nd. Females..................................

       3rd. Adults....................................

7. Number of prayer meetings attended?.................

8. Number of marriages solemnised?.....................

9. Number of sick visited in their homes?.................

10. Number of funerals attended?.......................

11. Number who have secured homes through your advice and help during the past week...........................

12. Does your S. S. use Sunday literature, such as books, quarterlies, S. S. papers, etc.? State which...............

       Sign here. (Name).............................

       (Home P. O. address)......................

       ....

☞ Please answer EVERY question, and return to E. J. Penny.

A volunteer prayer meeting is held daily, just after breakfast, in the Bible School building, under the guidance of the Bible students. This meeting is well attended by young men of all the classes, who take turns in leading the services.

Any one passing this building at that hour will hear songs of praise and earnest voices in prayer to God. All these societies, at Christmas and

Thanksgiving, unite in taking food and other comforts to the deserving poor and helpless.

All the young men and boys at Tuskegee are assigned to groups numbering twelve to fifteen, each group in charge of a teacher. There are eighty of these small companies formed that the boys may become better acquainted with one another, and grow in a spirit of mutual helpfulness. Every boy feels that he can go to the teacher who is in charge of his social unit for advice and comfort. This feature of the school life is under the general direction of the Chaplain, and has done much to make the students feel at home. Discipline has been more satisfactory since the plan was adopted. The young women students are organised in other ways to meet their own social and religious needs, and to bring them into personal relations with their teachers.

All these forces are working more and more for good, and the School is in an encouraging and healthy religious condition.

CHAPTER XVII

Some Tangible Results

Since the founding of the Tuskegee Normal and Industrial Institute, in 1881, the total enrollment of young men and women who have remained long enough to be helped, in any degree, is about six thousand. From the beginning, the school has sought to find out the chief occupations by which our people earn their living, and to train men and women to be of service in these callings. Those who go out follow the industries they have learned, or teach in public or private schools, teaching part of the year and farming or labouring the remainder of their time. Some follow house-keeping or other domestic service, while others enter professions, the Government service, or become merchants. Many of the teachers give instruction in agriculture, or in the industries. The professional men are largely physicians and the professional women are mostly trained nurses.

After diligent investigation I have been unable to find a dozen former students in idleness. They are busy in schoolroom, field, shop, home or church. They are busy because they have placed themselves in demand by learning to do that which the world wants done, and because they have learned the disgrace of idleness, and the sweetness of labour.   One of the greatest embarrassments which confronts our school at the present time is our inability to supply any large proportion of the demands for our students that are coming to us constantly from the people of both races, North and South.   But, apart from their skill and training, that which has made Tuskegee men and women succeed is their spirit of unselfishness and their willingness to sacrifice themselves for others.   In many cases while building up a struggling school in a community, they have worked for months without any fixed salary or promise of salary, because they have learned that helping some one else is the secret of happiness. Because of the demand for men and women trained at Tuskegee, it is difficult to keep a large proportion of the students in the school until they graduate. It is, therefore, not so easy to show the results of the work in concrete form as it would be if a larger number of the students finished.   But the facts obtainable prove that the school is achieving its purpose in preparing its students to do what the world wants done.

Some years ago a young man named Williams came to Tuskegee from Mobile, Alabama.   Before coming, he had nearly completed the public-school course of study at Mobile, and had been earning about fifty cents a day at various kinds of unskilled labour. He wished to study further in the academic branches, with the object of combining this knowledge with the trade of brick-masonry. To take the full course in brick-masonry, including mechanical drawing, he should have remained three years. He remained for six months only. During this time, he got some rough knowledge of brick-masonry and advanced somewhat in his academic studies. When he returned to Mobile, it soon became known that he had been working at brick-masonry. At once he was dubbed a full-fledged mason. As there was unusual building activity in Mobile at that time, he found himself in great demand, and, instead of having to seek odd jobs, he soon saw that, in spite of his rather crude knowledge of the trade, he could earn one dollar and fifty cents per day, and have more work offered him than he could do. When the three months' vacation expired, Williams debated whether he ought to return to Tuskegee to finish his course or remain at home and try to purchase a home for his widowed mother. Hence, seeing an opportunity to make two dollars a day *at his trade*, he decided not to return. As in hundreds of other cases, the Mobile man had unusual natural ability, and was able to get out of his six months at Tuskegee a mental, spiritual, and bodily awakening which fixed his purpose in life. Not only this, but he had made such a start in his trade that by close study and observation he was able to improve from month to month in the quantity and quality of his work, and within a few months he ceased to work for other people by the day and began to make small contracts. At the present time, Mr. Williams is one of the most substantial coloured citizens of Mobile. He owns his home and is a reliable and successful contractor, doing important work for both races. In addition to being a successful brick-mason and contractor, he owns and operates a dairy business, and his class of patronage is not limited by any means to members of the Negro race.

The value, then, of the work of schools, where the trade or economic element enters in so largely as it does at Tuskegee, cannot be judged in any large degree by the number of students who finish the full course and receive diplomas. What is true of the course in brick-masonry is true in larger or smaller measure of all the other thirty-seven industrial divisions of the school.

Another example: Crawford D. Menafee came to Tuskegee about 1890, and began taking the agricultural and academic courses. He was older than the average student, and entered one of the lower classes. Because he had no money to pay any part of his expenses, he was given permission to enter the night school, which meant that he was to work on the farm ten hours a day, receiving, meanwhile, lessons in the principles of farming and devoting two hours at night to the academic branches. He was never classed as a very bright student, and in the purely literary studies made such slow progress, after repeating several classes, that he left two years before completing either the agricultural or the academic course. It was noted, however, that, notwithstanding inability to grasp theoretical work, he manifested unusual enthusiasm and showed special ability in practical farm work. His ability was so marked that he was asked to take a place of responsibility as assistant to one of the school's farm managers. It soon became evident that he possessed extraordinary executive ability. He read constantly everything of value which he could secure upon agriculture, and soon began to show signs of considerable intellectual growth and the possession of a rarely systematic mind. Mr. Menafee was soon promoted to a higher position at Tuskegee.

A few years later, there came a call for some one to introduce theoretical and practical agriculture into the State Normal College for coloured people at Tallahassee, Florida. Mr. Menafee was recommended. The students had no wish to learn agriculture. They were opposed to it in any form. By tact and patience, Mr. Menafee gradually won the students and made them see the importance of intelligent cultivation of the soil. Mr. Menafee has now been in charge of the agricultural department of the Florida school for three years, and has made the study of theoretical and practical farming so effective that it is now one of the most popular branches in the school. Not only do the young men cultivate a large acreage each year, but a number of girls also receive instruction in gardening, dairying, and poultry raising. In a word, the whole attitude of the school toward agriculture has been revolutionised, and the department has been placed upon an effective and practical foundation.

There are hundreds of cases similar to those of Mr. Menafee and the Mobile brick-mason. These represent a class of students who have absorbed the spirit of the school as well as its methods, and who are doing far-reaching service, although they are not enrolled on our list of graduates. We have tried to give special attention to all forms of agricultural training at Tuskegee, because we believe that the Negro, like any other race in a similar stage of development, is better off when owning and cultivating the soil.

As I have explained elsewhere, the results of our agricultural work in the past have not been as manifest as they will be in the future, for the Institute has been compelled to give foremost place to the building trades in order to get under shelter. The task of erecting nearly seventy buildings, in which to house about seventeen hundred people, has not been easy And yet what are some of the results of our lessons in farming? Not long ago I drove through a section of Macon County, Alabama. My drive extended a distance of perhaps eight miles, and during this time I passed through or near the farms of A. H. Adams, Thomas Courrier, Frank McCay, Nathaniel Harris, Thomas Anderson, John Smith, and Dennis Upshaw. These seven men had attended the Tuskegee Institute for longer or shorter periods, and each had already paid for his farm or was buying it. All of these men had studied in the Phelps Hall Bible Training School in the morning, and had taken the agricultural course in the afternoon. When I visited their farms, I saw them actually at work, and it was most encouraging and interesting to note the air of cleanliness and system about their farms and homes. In every case they were not confining themselves to the raising of cotton, but had learned to diversify their crops. All were active in church and Sunday-school work, and were using their influence to get others to buy homes. The most prosperous farmer among them was Mr. Upshaw. He began farming with practically nothing. At present he owns one hundred and fifteen acres of land, which is cultivated by himself and family. On this land is a neat, attractive house, a barn and outbuildings, and a small sugar house for boiling syrup from the cane which he raises for his own use. His home and farm are models for other farmers. He raises not only cotton, but corn and oats, vegetables, fruit, live stock, and fowls.

He has an unusually fine peach orchard. Mr. and Mrs. Upshaw are leaders in the County Farmers' Institute. Mrs. Upshaw is also a member of the Mothers' Meeting, which assembles regularly in the town of Tuskegee. While Mr. Upshaw's present house is better than the average farmhouse in that section, when I last visited this farm, I found lumber on the ground to be used in erecting a new and larger house. Hundreds of such examples could be cited.

I have given these seven examples because people who know absolutely nothing about the subject often make the statement that when a Negro gets any degree of education he will not work—especially as a farmer. As a rule, people who make these sweeping assertions against the Negro are blinded by prejudice. The judgment of any man, black or white, who is controlled by race prejudice is not to be trusted. With one exception, I did not know of the farming operations of these men before the drive referred to; but I was not at all surprised at what I saw, because my years of experience have brought me into unbroken contact with Tuskegee men and women all over the South, and wherever I have met them I have found that they had in some degree raised the level of life about them.

Another branch of Agriculture, to which we have for a number of years given special attention, is dairying. The demand from Southern white people

for trained dairymen is much greater than we have
been able to supply.

In 1898, L. A. Smith finished the course of training in dairying and in the academic branches. He
had been able to complete his course only by working
during the day and attending school at night during
the greater part of his time here. Soon after Smith
graduated, we had a call for a well-trained dairyman
from the Forest City Creamery Company, Rockford,
Illinois. Smith was recommended. He has been
holding an important position in the creamery for
five years, and has several times been promoted with
an increase of salary. Smith has paid for a neat
and comfortable home, and he has the confidence
and respect of the entire community. He looked
so young and inexperienced in taking up his work
that his ability was doubted, but it did not take him
long to prove that he was fully equal to the occasion.
The proprietor unhesitatingly said that he was one
of the most proficient and valuable men in his
employ, and that he had placed him in a very important and trying position—that of making butter
cultures. This is a secret department in which no
one except the employees operating it and the
proprietor is permitted to enter. Mr. Smith also
did some important chemical work in connection
with a lawsuit supposed to involve the manufacture
of spurious butter.

In Montgomery County, Alabama, Mr. N. N.

Scott, a Southern white man, has operated for a number of years the largest and most successful dairy farm in his section. Mr. Scott has in his employ three Tuskegee men, with Scott Thomas in charge. Mr. Scott tells us that those men trained at our school are the most efficient helpers he can secure. He keeps a standing order with Mr. George W. Carver, our instructor in dairying, to the effect that he will employ any one that Mr. Carver recommends. Not far from Mr. Scott's dairy is a smaller one owned by Mr. E. J. Hughes, another white man. Some time ago Mr. Hughes secured Luther M. Jones, who had taken only a partial course in dairying at Tuskegee, to make butter and cheese for him. Such examples can be found in nearly every one of the Southern States.

From the beginning, the work of this institution has been closely related to the public school system of the South, for it must be clear to all that in the last analysis we must depend upon public schools for the general education of the masses, and it is important that the larger institutions for the education of the Negro keep in close and sympathetic touch with the school officials of the Southern States.

One way in which we assist the public school system of the South is by sending out men and women who become the teachers of teachers. One of the best examples of this is the case of Isaac Fisher, a young man who came to Tuskegee a number of years ago, and earned his board by working during the day and going to school at night. Two years ago Mr. Fisher, upon my recommendation, was elected by the State officials of the State of Arkansas to the important position of Principal of the Branch Normal College of Pine Bluff, Arkansas, the main institution for training coloured teachers for the public schools of that commonwealth. Mr. Fisher has associated with him a large force of teachers, two of whom also are Tuskegee graduates. In the school are students many of whom will become not only public-school teachers in the usual sense, but having been trained by Mr. Fisher in the industries, they will be able to introduce them gradually into their teaching. There is hardly a single Southern State where our men and women are not found in some of the larger schools for training teachers.

Our students at Tuskegee are instructed constantly in methods of building schoolhouses and prolonging the school term. It is safe to say that outside the larger Southern cities and towns in the rural district, one will find nine-tenths of the school buildings wholly unfit for use, and rarely is the public school session longer than five months—in most cases not more than four. These conditions exist largely because of the poverty of the States. One of the problems of our teachers is to show the people how through private effort they can build schoolhouses and extend the school term.

Milton Calloway left Tuskegee three years ago. In addition to taking the normal course, he learned the trade of tinsmithing. When he returned to his home at Union Spring, Bullock County, Alabama, he secured a school some distance in the country. The term was so short that Calloway found he could not live all the year by teaching during the three or four months of the session. Calloway's trade came to his rescue. Soon after he began teaching, he made an arrangement with a white man in the town by which he was to work in his shop on Saturdays and during his vacation months. By following this plan, the school is gradually being built up, the people are being taught to save their money, improve the school-house, prolong the school term, and buy homes.

Moses P. Simmons, another one of our graduates in an adjoining county, has lengthened the term of the public school by teaching the children how to grow vegetables, which have been disposed of for school purposes.

During the latest session of our Negro Conference in February, one delegate from Conecuh County, Alabama, told how his people had nearly doubled the length of the school term by each family's agreeing to plant an extra half-acre which was designated as the "school half-acre." A number of Tuskegee men and women have put on foot some such scheme as this.

I asked one of the officials of the Tuskegee Institute to canvass our nearest large city, Montgomery, Alabama, in order to obtain the name of every student there who had received a diploma or certificate from Tuskegee, or who had remained long enough to be in any degree influenced by its teaching, and to report to me exactly what he found after making a personal inspection.   Here are a few of his reports:

"Perry, J. W., class of 1889, lives near the city. Is farming.   He controls 150 acres, owns five head of cattle, and teaches school six months in the year.

"Davis, Joseph, who has been away from Tuskegee three years, I found at work on a four-story building in process of erection on Commerce Street. He was getting $2.50 a day.   At work on the same job were William Fuller at $3.60 a day, and H. T. Wheat at $2.50.   Last summer Fuller received $4 a day for four months, at Troy, Alabama.

"Moten, Pierce, is at work as drug clerk in the drug store of D. A. C. Dungee, at the corner of Court and Washington Streets.   He graduated from Tuskegee in 1902.   While at the school he worked in the hospital, and much of that time had charge of the drug room.   He is studying medicine, and has already spent a session at Meharry Medical College, Nashville, Tennessee.

"Campbell, Mrs. Berry N. (Miss Bowen), graduated in the class of 1887, and her home has been in Montgomery most of the time since then, although her work at times takes her away from the city.   She is a trained nurse of excellent reputation and wide experience, and has frequently been employed at Hale's Infirmary. When I inquired for her she was taking care of a private case. She owns two good houses on Union Street and on High Street, both of which I saw. She also owns a vacant lot."

There were only three whose records were found to be uncertain or unsatisfactory. The same kind of investigation will reveal almost similar conditions existing in a greater or less degree in other Southern cities.

Now let me show their life in smaller towns: one containing between four and five thousand inhabitants. Some time ago Mr. Bedford, one of our trustees, made a personal investigation in Eufaula, Alabama. I quote directly from Mr. Bedford as to what he found:

"Sydney Murphy graduated in 1887. He went at once to Eufaula. For three years he taught and farmed in the country. He was then made principal of the coloured public schools of the city. He still holds this position, and is now serving his thirteenth year. He has a nice home in the city, three houses that he rents, and some vacant lots.

"John Jordan, 1901, a graduate in harness-making, opened a shop in Eufaula, September, 1901. He reached Eufaula with $16 and a very few tools. He paid $7 license, $3.50 in advance for a month's rent, and had $5.50 for board and other expenses.

He curtained off a little space in his shop for a bedroom, and with an oilstove cooked his own meals.
In this way he saved up $50, but lost it in the failure
of the bank of Eufaula. He has gone right on with
his business, and now has one of the best shops in
the city. He has established the People's Library,
which has more than 600 volumes in it. He has a
reading-room and literary society over which he
presides, and is superintendent of the A. M. E.
Sunday-school."

After several years at the school, during which
they worked upon the school farm, Frank and
Dow L. Reid left Tuskegee at the completion of
the B Middle Class. Frank, the older brother, left
in the year 1888, and Dow in the year 1891. Before
coming to Tuskegee, these young men had lived
upon a rented farm with their father, but on returning home they decided to buy a farm of their
own. They entered into an agreement to purchase
a farm of 320 acres, four miles from the old home-
stead, and with little or no money, but with a
determination to succeed, they began to cultivate
the land. They agreed to pay $5.50 per acre for
the place, and, regardless of the fact that they had
little money at the time, they bought the farm,
paying in a few years the whole amount, $1,760.
In addition to this farm, the Reid brothers, as they
are styled for miles around, have bought another
farm of 225 acres at $10 per acre. This farm is

about two miles away from the place first mentioned. When the final payment upon this last purchase is made in the fall, after crops have been gathered and marketed, a total of $4,010 will have been made and expended for land by these young men since the younger one left Tuskegee some twelve years ago.

The stock and farming implements on these farms are far superior to those seen upon most of the plantations. On the farm of 320 acres are seventeen fine horses and mules, all large and in good condition; there are thirty well-bred cows and fifty fine, healthy looking hogs, besides a large number of chickens and guineas, which furnish plenty of eggs for the families' use. The farming implements, including plows, mowers, rakes, harrows, etc., are of the latest patterns. The four double wagons, the single top-buggy, the road wagon and go-cart are all in good order, and are kept under cover when not in use. We often find farmers in the South who, when the crop is made, leave the plows, the mower, the rake, in fact, all the farming implements, standing out in the field, exposed to wind and weather all through the winter months. A visitor to the Reid brothers' plantation will find that each piece of machinery on this plantation has a place under a shed built for the purpose, and is kept there when not in use.

There are eight dwelling-houses—a four-room

frame building in which the young men and their families live, and seven log cabins in which the farmhands live with their families. The first is rather old and uncomely in appearance from the outside, but the interior is more pleasing. The bedrooms are large and clean, with sufficient windows and doors to permit of necessary ventilation during the sleeping hours. The dining-room is well kept, and the whole interior of the house presents a neat, clean and attractive appearance. This house is to be replaced by a larger one, to be built during the winter.

A large cotton-gin, with an eighty-tooth saw, is owned and operated by these young men. Last year, besides ginning the 125 bales of cotton raised upon their own plantation, they ginned the cotton raised by nearly all the other farmers in the neighbourhood.

The post-office at Dawkins was formerly about four miles from its present location, but since the Reid brothers settled there and the community grew so rapidly the post-office was removed to their place, and the plantation was named Dawkins. The post-office is located in the general merchandise store of the Reids, and Mr. Frank Reid is postmaster. There was neither a church nor a schoolhouse in the community when these young men went to Dawkins. They purchased four acres of land nearby, and not only gave this land, but assisted in building a comfortable church, which has been used both as a church and a schoolhouse. Preaching services are held regularly in the church, and a flourishing school is taught from seven to nine months each year. Last year more than one hundred boys and girls were registered.

Mr. J. N. Calloway, who graduated from the Tuskegee Institute in 1892, is principal of the school, and has one assistant teacher. A new two-room schoolhouse is now being built through the efforts of Mr. Calloway, and will be completed at the time of the opening of the school the latter part of next October.

I am often asked to what extent we are able to supply domestic servants directly from this institution. I always answer, "Not to any large extent, notwithstanding the fact that women are trained here in everything relating to work in the home." When a woman finishes one of our courses, she is in demand at once at a salary three or four times as large as that paid in the average home. Aside from this, we are doing a larger service by sending out over a large extent of territory strong leaders who will go into local communities and teach the lessons of home-making than we could by trying to send a cook directly into each family who applies to us. The latter would be a never-ending process. Miss Annie Canty, for example, teaches cooking and other industries in the public schools of Columbus, Georgia.

There is a little leaven that we hope will gradually help leaven the whole lump. Largely through the influence of our graduates, cooking and other industries are being taught in many of the public schools of the South. Another young woman, Miss Mary L. McCrary, is doing the same thing in the Industrial College for coloured people in Oklahoma.

Not a few of our men have become merchants, and they are generally patronised by both races and have high commercial rating. Two of the best examples of this class are Mr. A. J. Wilborn, who is a successful merchant in the town of Tuskegee, and Mr. A. J. Wood, of Benton, Alabama.

Last January, when in Los Angeles, California, I met by chance a young man who had taken a partial course in our nurse-training department. I asked him if he were reflecting credit upon the Tuskegee Institute? Without a word, he pulled out a bank-book and asked me to inspect it. I found a substantial sum recorded to his credit. Before I was through with the inspection of the first bank-book, he handed me a second which showed an amount to his credit at another bank. I found that Mrs. Barre, another of our graduates, is one of the leading trained nurses of the same city.

CHAPTER XVIII

SPREADING THE TUSKEGEE SPIRIT

ONE of the questions most frequently asked me is, To what extent are Tuskegee graduates able to reproduce the work of the parent institution? Just as the Tuskegee Institute is an outgrowth of the Hampton Institute, so other smaller schools have grown out of the Tuskegee Institute in various parts of the country. There are at present sixteen schools of some size which have grown out of the Tuskegee Institute or have been organised by Tuskegee men and women. In all instances, these schools have become large enough to be chartered under the laws of the State.

The Vorhees Industrial School at Denmark, South Carolina, for example, was founded by Elizabeth E. Wright, class of 1894. It is now in its seventh year. Miss Wright was greatly opposed at first by both the white and coloured people, but she persevered, and has at length overcome all opposition. She has 300 acres of land, all paid for. A large central building has been erected at a cost of $3,000. This contains offices, class rooms, and a chapel that will seat 600. This building is paid for, and a girls' dormitory, to cost $4,000, the money for which is in the treasury, is in process of erection. The plans for both of these buildings were drawn by a Tuskegee student. A barn to cost $800 is nearly completed, and there are several other small buildings. Miss Wright is assisted by three Tuskegee graduates, one as the farm superintendent, one as treasurer and bookkeeper, and the other as carpenter and teacher of drawing. The day and boarding students number more than 300. Farming in its various branches is the principal work of the students, but they are also taught shoemaking, carpentry, cooking, sewing, housekeeping, and laundering, while printing and blacksmithing are soon to be added to the course. The school spent $9,000 last year in current expenses, building expenses, and the purchase of land.

Another of our graduates, Mr. V. Chambliss, has charge of the farming operations of the Southern Land Improvement Company. About forty Negro families have settled upon land controlled by this organisation, and the number is increasing each year. These families are being given the opportunity to buy their homes through their own labour and under the guidance of Mr. Chambliss. Mr. Chambliss does not use the hoe himself, for he finds it more economical to utilise his time directing the work. When the world wants cotton or corn, it cares little whether the man uses his pen or his hoe. What it desires are results. Some men have the ability to produce fifty times as much cotton with the pen as with the hoe. Another example will show how our students succeed when working directly under others. The letter which follows is to the point:

PROFESSOR BOOKER T. WASHINGTON.

Dear Sir: The students from your school who have been at work here during the vacation expect to return to Tuskegee to-morrow, and we want to say to you that these boys have demonstrated to our company the wonderful benefit of your teaching. These young men have taken hold of their work in a steady and businesslike way, and have worked uncomplainingly during the severe heat of the past summer. We would like, if it is possible, to induce a number of your students to purchase their homes about our works in North Birmingham and become regular workmen in our different shops. We have a letter before us now, written by one of your students, John Davis, which would reflect credit on the masters of Yale or Harvard. Please accept our best wishes for the success of the grand work you have undertaken.

DIMMICK PIPE WORKS COMPANY,
Birmingham, Alabama.

A conspicuous example of a Tuskegee graduate who is using his knowledge of stock-raising in a practical way is that of William Johnson Shoals, of Clear Creek, Indian Territory. Shoals owns and operates his own stock farm, one of the largest in the Territory, and has been successful from the very beginning.

The following letter indicates one of the ways in which we are able to assist the public-school system from time to time:

ETHELVILLE, ALABAMA, June, 1903.
PROFESSOR B. T. WASHINGTON.

I am very anxious to afford the coloured teachers of this county the best instruction possible, and so I write to ask if you
cannot send us one of your teachers to conduct a Normal Institute, to be held at Carrollton, June 29th to July 4th—a teacher
whom you can recommend.   I am sorry to say the county has
no money it can spend on this matter.

Yours truly,
W. H. STOREY,
County Superintendent of Education.

The following institutions have grown out of the
Tuskegee Institute and have been chartered under
the laws of their respective States.   Not only have
they been founded by Tuskegee graduates, but the
officers and in many cases the entire faculty are
from Tuskegee:

Mt. Meigs Institute, Waugh, Alabama; Snow Hill
Institute, Snow Hill, Alabama; Vorhees Industrial
School, Denmark, South Carolina; East Tennessee
Normal and Industrial Institute, Harriman, Ten-
nessee;   Robert Hungerford Industrial Institute,
Eatonville, Florida; Topeka Educational and Indus-
trial Institute, Topeka, Kansas; Allengreene Normal
and Industrial Institute, Ruston, Louisiana; Utica
Normal and Industrial Institute, Mississippi; Chris-
tianburg Institute, Cambria, Virginia.

The story of struggle, sacrifice and hard work
connected with the founding of some of these schools
is more akin to romance than to reality.

Snow Hill Institute, Snow Hill, Alabama, by way

A FURNITURE AND REPAIR SHOP AT SNOW HILL.

of illustration, was founded by William J. Edwards, of the class of 1893. This school is now in its tenth year, and was started in a one-room cabin. Soon after the school was established, Honourable R. O. Simpson, a wealthy white resident of the community, was so impressed with its good effect upon the Negroes of the vicinity that he gave the school forty acres of land. This has been added to, until the school now owns 160 acres, and property to the value of $30,000.

Last year it expended $20,000 in its operations. It has about 400 students, 200 of them being boarding students. The following trades are taught: Farming, carpentry, wheelwrighting, blacksmithing, painting, brickmaking, printing, sewing, cooking, housekeeping. About twenty teachers and instructors are employed, nearly all graduates or former students of Tuskegee. Snow Hill has sent out twenty-five graduates. All are required to pass the State teachers' examination before graduating. Six of them are teachers in the Institute. The school not only has the support and the sympathy of Mr. R. O. Simpson, but of all the best white people in the county.

A little more than a year ago one of our graduates, Mr. Charles P. Adams, established a small school at Ruston, Louisiana. At present the school owns twenty-five acres of land, on which a schoolhouse costing $1,200 has been built and paid for. The school term has been extended from three to eight months, with three teachers—all Tuskegee graduates—and 110 pupils. In connection with the class-room work the students are taught agriculture and housekeeping. All this has been done in a little more than one year with money and labour contributed by the people of both races in the community. In regard to Mr. Adams's work, Honourable B. F. Thompson, the Mayor of Ruston, says, "Professor Adams deserves credit for what he has accomplished." Honourable S. D. Pearce, the representative of the parish in the State Legislature, says, "The school is doing fine work for the education of the coloured youth of this section of the State, and Professor Adams is making a vigorous struggle for its advancement." Mr. W. E. Redwine, Superintendent of Public Instruction for the parish, says, "Professor Adams is doing work in the right direction for the betterment of his race." Mr. A. J. Bell, the editor of the local newspaper, says, "His work in this section has been productive of incalculable good."

As to the work of the Utica Normal and Industrial Institute, Utica, Mississippi, I will let Mr. W. H. Holtzclaw, the principal, tell in his own words:

"I came here from Snow Hill, Alabama, last October, without a cent (I left my wife behind because of lack of means to bring her, and I walked part of the way through a wild and unfrequented part of this State), and started this work under a tree. Now

A SEWING-CLASS AT SNOW HILL

we have two horses, forty acres of land, one cow and a calf, a farm planted and growing, more than 200 students, seven teachers, and a building going up. In all my efforts I have had the wise counsel and constant assistance of Mrs. Holtzclaw, without which I could not have made much progress."

Harriman Industrial Institute, Harriman, Tennessee, was established five years ago by J. W. Oveltrea, of the class of 1893. The school has thirty acres of land in the suburbs of Harriman. Mr. Oveltrea and his wife are both graduates of Tuskegee, and they have been aided in their work by Tuskegee graduates and students. The school has four buildings and about one hundred students. Several trades are taught.

The Robert Hungerford Institute, in Eatonville, Florida, was founded by R. C. Calhoun, of the class of 1896. Eatonville is about six miles from Orlando. Mr. Calhoun had nothing to begin with but the little public school. He has secured 200 acres of land, clear of debt, and a year ago dedicated Booker T. Washington Hall, a dormitory and classroom building, with chapel. This building, the plans of which were drawn by a Tuskegee graduate, cost $3,000. The trades taught are farming, wheelwrighting, painting, carpentry, sewing, cooking and laundering.

Miss Nathalie Lord, one of my early teachers at Hampton, is a trustee of this school. The school is now in its fourth year.   It has forty boarding students and nearly one hundred day students.   Mrs. Calhoun, who is her husband's assistant, was a student at Tuskegee, as was also the man who has charge of the blacksmith and wheelwright shops.

Nearly three years ago, three of our graduates, under the leadership of one of our teachers, Mr. J. N. Calloway, went to Africa under the auspices of the German government, to introduce cotton-raising among the natives.   At the end of the second year the German officials were so pleased that they employed three other students.   At the end of the fourth year the experiment was successful to the extent that a hundred bales of cotton have been shipped from the colony of Togo, Africa, to Berlin. Only a few months ago the German officials were kind enough to send me several pairs of hose made from cotton raised by our students.

Since beginning this experiment, we have received applications from both English and Belgian cotton-raising companies that wish to secure Tuskegee men to introduce cotton-raising in their African possessions.   The Porto Rican Government makes an annual appropriation for the purpose of maintaining eighteen students at Tuskegee in order that they may learn our methods.   The Haytian Government has recently arranged to send a number of young men here, mainly with the view of their being trained in farming.   Besides, we have students present from the West Indies, Africa, and several South American countries.

While speaking of the Tuskegee missionary spirit, it is interesting to note the effect that the industrial training given by our graduates has had upon the morals and manner of living among the natives of Africa in Togoland. Missionaries have been working among these people for many years, and very effectively, and yet training in carpentry and cotton-raising had results that the academic and religious teaching had not accomplished. When the natives are taught the Bible, and the heart and the head are educated, the tendency is for them to become teachers or traders. In the latter case, their learning brings them too frequently into contact with unscrupulous European traders from whom they acquire habits of gambling, cheating, drinking, etc. In addition to this, when they begin *merchandising*, the natives find that it is to their advantage to have more than one wife, since their wives are able to help them in selling in the markets and through the country districts. The young people who went to Africa from Tuskegee found that this problem greatly perplexed the missionaries, but wherever these natives were given work on the plantations, and employed their muscles as well as their brains, a change for the better was soon apparent.

It is usually true that when a native is kept employed in one place, he will begin to build a home,

consisting of a number of huts; he will clear a farm
or plantation, and stock it with cattle, sheep, pigs
and fowls.   He will plant vegetables, corn, cassava,
yams, etc.   This happened among the Africans who
were employed on the plantations cultivated by our
graduates.   The wives and children of these labour-
ers were given work on the farms, and it has been
found that few of them gamble, steal and cheat, as
do those who wander to and fro without employment.   Such natives as these cotton-growers are
more easily reached by missionary effort, and when
they are converted to the Christian religion, if they
remain on the farms, they seldom fall back into
paganism.

I have been informed that it is a general opinion
among the missionaries in Togoland that industrial
education will be a main-stay in future effort, and
that such teaching will be introduced in the missionary institutions as rapidly as possible.   Since the
young men went out from Tuskegee, a decided
change has been noticed in the sanitation and mode
of living in the towns near which they are located.
Much of this betterment has been the direct result
of the lessons learned by the natives from seeing our
carpenter build houses, and observing our graduates'
habits of life.   The natives seemed anxious to learn,
and the Tuskegee colony received many applications
from the women to have their daughters come and
live with the American women in order that they

might learn the new customs, especially the art of
sewing, cooking, and doing housework.

Few of the huts had shutters or doors when our
graduates first went to the colony—bedsteads were
unknown; but now many of the huts have outside
shutters, and their inmates have learned how to
construct comfortable beds for themselves. Many
who formerly bathed in streams now have bath-
houses back of their huts. On Sunday, all work on
the plantations of the Tuskegee party was sus-
pended, except caring for the stock and other necessary duties, and this, too, had its effect on the
natives, who were inclined to accept our religious
observance of the day. Many now dress in holiday
attire on Sunday, and go to the nearest mission.

The Tuskegee party settled about sixty miles
from the coast, where no wagons or carts were used
for conveying produce or material. The native men
and women carried all freight in sixty-pound loads
on their heads, and were able to travel fifteen to
twenty miles a day. On these round trips of ten
days, the women carried their small children with
them, and during their frequent halts came into contact with the rough and demoralising element of the
trading-post, and with other degrading influences.
This mode of transportation seemed very unsatisfactory to the Tuskegee young men, who introduced
carts and wagons drawn by men. This allowed the
women and children to remain at home and look

after the farms and their household duties, while the men made the trips to the coast.

Young girls, just growing into womanhood, are no longer compelled to meet the many bad influences formerly encountered on the trips to the coast. The use of farm machinery in the colony has relieved the women and girls of much drudgery. They used to prepare the land with the crudest hoes and plows. This is now done with improved American implements. The Germans have been so strongly impressed with these effects of industrial training upon the natives, that they have decided to introduce into all the schools of that colony a system for the training of boys in hand work. With the assistance of the chiefs, improved methods of agriculture and handicraft will be spread among the tribes of that region.

I do not wish my readers to get the impression that all of Tuskegee's men and women have succeeded, because they have not. A few have failed miserably, much to our regret, but the percentage of failures is so small that they are more than overshadowed by those who have been, in the fullest sense of the word, successful.

Despite all that I have said, the work has merely begun. I believe we have found the way. Our endeavour will be to continue to pursue it faithfully, actively, bravely, honestly. With sufficient means, such work as I have indicated could be greatly increased.

CHAPTER XIX

Negro Education Not a Failure

Several persons holding high official position have said recently that it does not pay, from any point of view, to educate the Negro; and that all attempts at his education have so far failed to accomplish any good results. The Southern States, which out of their poverty are contributing rather liberally for the education of all the people, as does individual and organised philanthropy throughout the country, have a right to know whether the Negro is responding to the efforts they have made to place him upon a higher plane òf civilisation.

Will it pay to invest further money in this direction? In seeking to answer this question, it is hardly fair to compare the progress of the American Negro with that of the American white man, who, in some unexplained way, got thousand of years ahead of the Negro in the arts and sciences of civilisation. But to get at the real facts and the real capability of the black man, compare for a moment the American Negro with the Negro in Africa, or the black man with the black man. In South Africa alone there are five million black people who have never been brought, through school or other agencies, into contact with a higher civilisation in a way to have their minds or their ambitions strengthened or awakened. As a result, the industries of South Africa languish and refuse to prosper for lack of labour. The native black man refuses to labour because he has been neglected. He has few wants and little ambition, and these can be satisfied by labouring one or two days out of the seven. In the southern part of the United States there are more than eight millions of my race who, both by contact with the whites and by education in the home, in school, in church, have had their minds awakened and strengthened—have thus had their wants increased and multiplied many times. Hence, instead of a people in idleness, we have in the South a people who are anxious to work because they want education for their children; they want land and houses, and churches, books, and papers. In a word, they want the highest and best in our civilisation. Looked at, then, from the most material and selfish point of view, it has paid to awaken the Negro's mind, and there should be no limit placed upon the development of that mind.

Does the American Negro take advantage of opportunities to secure education? Practically no schoolhouse has been opened for the Negro since the war that has not been filled. Often hungry and in rags, making heroic sacrifices, the Negro youth has been determined to annihilate his mental darkness. With all his disadvantages, the Negro, according to official records, has blotted out 55.5 per cent. of his illiteracy since he became a free man, while practically 95 per cent. of the native Africans are illiterate. After years of civilisation and opportunity, in Spain, 68 per cent. of the population are illiterate; in Italy, 38 per cent. In the average South American country about 80 per cent. are illiterate, while after forty years the American Negro has only 44.5 per cent. of illiteracy to his debit. I have thus compared the progress of my race, not with the highest civilised nations, for the reason that, in passing judgment upon us, the world too often forgets that, either consciously or otherwise, because of geographical or physical proximity to the American white man, we are being compared with the very highest civilisation that exists. But when compared with the most advanced and enlightened white people of the South, we find 12 per cent. of illiteracy for them and only 44 per cent. for our race.

Having seen that the American Negro takes advantage of every opportunity to secure an education, I think it will surprise some to learn to what an extent the race contributes toward its own education and works in sympathetic touch with the whites at the South. In emphasising this fact, I use the testimony of the best Southern white men. Says the State Superintendent of Education of Florida in one of his recent official reports: "The following figures are given to show that the education of the Negroes of Middle Florida (the Black Belt of Florida) does not cost the white people of that section one cent." In those eight Black Belt counties, the total cost of the Negro schools is $19,457. The total contributed by the Negro in direct and indirect taxes amounted to $23,984, thus leaving a difference of $4,527, which, according to the Superintendent, went into the white schools. In Mississippi, for the year ending in 1899, according to an eminent authority, the Negroes had expended on their schools about 20 per cent. of the total school fund, or a total of about $250,000. During the same year they paid toward their own education, in poll taxes, State, county and city taxes, and indirect taxes, about $280,000, or a surplus of about $30,000. So that, looked at from any point of view, it would seem that the Negroes in that State are in a large measure paying for their own education.

But with all the Negro is doing for himself, with all the white people in the South are doing for themselves, and despite all that one race is doing to help the other, the present opportunities for education are woefully inadequate for both races. In the year 1877–78 the total expenditure for education in the ex-slave States was a beggarly $2.61 per capita for whites and only $1.09 for blacks; on the same basis the U. S. Commissioner of Education calculates that

TYPESETTING—PRINTING OFFICE

for the year 1900–01, $35,400,000 was spent for the education of both races in the South, of which $6,000,000 went to Negroes, or $4.92 per capita for whites and $2.21 for blacks. On the same basis, each child in Massachusetts costs the taxpayers for its education $22.35, and each one in New York $20.53 yearly.

From both a moral and religious point of view, what measure of education the Negro has received has been repaid, and there has been no step backward in any State. Not a single graduate of the Hampton Institute or of the Tuskegee Institute can be found to-day in any jail or State penitentiary. After making careful inquiry, I cannot find a half-dozen cases of a man or woman who has completed a full course of education in any of our reputable institutions like Hampton, Tuskegee, Fisk or Atlanta, who are in prisons. The records of the South show that 90 per cent. of the coloured people in prisons are without knowledge of trades, and 61 per cent. are illiterate. This statement alone disproves the assertion that the Negro grows in crime as education increases. If the Negro at the North is more criminal than his brother at the South, it is because of the employment which the South gives him and the North denies him. It is not the educated Negro who has been guilty of or even charged with crime in the South; it is, as a rule, the one who has a mere smattering of education or is in total ignorance. While the Negro may succeed in getting into the State prison faster, the white man in some inexplainable manner has a way of getting out faster than the Negro. To illustrate: the official records of Virginia for a year show that one out of every three and one-half white men were freed from prison by executive clemency, and that only one out of every fourteen Negroes received such clemency. In Louisiana it is one to every four and one-half white men and one to every forty-nine Negroes. So that, when this feature is considered, matters are pretty well evened up between the races.

As bearing further upon the tendency of education to improve the morals of the Negro and therefore to prolong his life, no one will accuse the average New York insurance company of being guided by mere sentiment toward the Negro in placing its risks; with the insurance company it is a question of cold business. A few months ago the chief medical examiner for the largest industrial insurance company in America stated that, after twenty years' experience and observation, his company had found that the Negro who was intelligent, who worked regularly at a trade or some industry and owned his home, was as safe an insurance risk as a white man in the same station of life.

Not long ago, a Southern white man residing in the town of Tuskegee, who represents one of the largest and most wealthy accident and casualty companies in New York, wrote to his company to the effect that while he knew his company refused to insure the ordinary, ignorant coloured man, at the Tuskegee Institute there were some 150 officers and instructors who were persons of education and skill, with property and character, and that he, a Southern white man, advised that they be insured on the same terms as other races, and within a week the answer came back, "Insure without hesitation every Negro on the Tuskegee Institute grounds of the type you name." The fact is, that almost every insurance company is now seeking the business of the educated Negro. If education increased the risk, they would seek the ignorant Negro rather than the educated one. As bearing further upon the effect of education upon the morals of the Negro during the last forty years, let us go into the heart of the Black Belt of Mississippi and inquire of Alfred Holt Stone, a large and intelligent cotton planter, as to the progress of the race. Mr. Stone says: "The last census shows that the Negro constitutes 87.6 per cent. of the population of the Yazoo-Mississippi delta. Yet we hear of no black incubus; we have had few midnight assassinations, and fewer lynchings. The violation by a Negro of the person of a white woman is with us an unknown crime; nowhere else is the line marking the social separation of the two races more rigidly drawn; nowhere are the relations between the two more kindly. With us, race riots are un-

known, and we have but one Negro problem—
though that constantly confronts us—how to secure
more Negroes."

There are few higher authorities on the progress
of the Negro than Joel Chandler Harris, of the
Atlanta Constitution. Mr. Harris had opportunity
to know the Negro before the war, and he has followed his progress closely in freedom. In a statement published recently Mr. Harris says:

"In spite of all, however, the condition of the
Negro has been growing better.   . . . . .

"We cannot fairly judge a race, or a country, or a
religious institution, or a social organisation, or
society itself, nay, not the republic in which we take
pride, unless we measure it by the standard set up
by the men who are its best representatives.

"We are in such a furious hurry. We are placed
in a position of expecting a race but a few years from
inevitable ignorance imposed on it by the conditions
of slavery to make the most remarkable progress
that the world has ever heard of, and when we discover that in the nature of things this is impossible,
we shake our heads sadly and are ready to lose heart
and hope.

"The point I desire to make is that the over-
whelming majority of the Negroes in all parts of the
South, especially in the agricultural regions, are
leading sober and industrious lives. A temperate
race is bound to be industrious, and the Negroes are

temperate when compared with the whites. Even in the towns the majority of them are sober and industrious. The idle and criminal classes among them make a great show in the police court records, but right here in Atlanta the respectable and decent Negroes far outnumber those who are on the lists of the police as old or new offenders. I am bound to conclude from what I see all about me, and from what I know of the race elsewhere, that the Negro, notwithstanding the late start he has made in civilisation and enlightenment, is capable of making himself a useful member in the communities in which he lives and moves, and that he is becoming more and more desirous of conforming to all the laws that have been enacted for the protection of society."

Some time ago I sent out letters to representative Southern men, covering each ex-slave state, asking them, judging by their observation in their own communities, what effect education had upon the Negro. To those questions I received 136 replies as follows:

1. Has education made the Negro a more useful citizen?

Answers: Yes, 121; no, 4; unanswered, 11.

2. Has it made him more economical and more inclined to acquire wealth?

Answers: Yes, 98; no, 14; unanswered, 24.

3. Does it make him a more valuable workman, especially where skill and thought are required?

Answers: Yes, 132; no, 2; unanswered, 2.

4. Do well-trained, skilled Negro workmen find any difficulty in securing work in your community?

Answers: No, 117; yes, 4; unanswered, 15.

5. Are coloured men in business patronised by the whites in your community?

Answers: Yes, 92; no, 9; unanswered, 35. (The large number of cases in which this question was not answered is due to scarcity of business men.)

6. Is there any opposition to the coloured people's buying land in your community?

Answers: No, 128; yes, 3; unanswered, 5.

7. Has education improved the morals of the black race?

Answers: Yes, 97; no, 20; unanswered, 19.

8. Has it made his religion less emotional and more practical?

Answers: Yes, 101; no, 16; unanswered, 19.

9. Is it, as a rule, the ignorant or the educated who commit crime?

Answers: Ignorant, 115; educated, 3; unanswered, 17.

10. Does crime grow less as education increases among the coloured people?

Answers: Yes, 102; no, 19; unanswered, 15.

11. Is the moral growth of the Negro equal to his mental growth?

Answers: Yes, 55; no, 46; unanswered, 35.

But it has been said that the Negro proves economically valueless in proportion as he is educated. All will agree that the Negro in Virginia, for example, began life forty years ago in complete poverty, scarcely owning clothing or a day's food. From an economic point of view, what has been accomplished for Virginia alone largely through the example and work of the graduates of Hampton and other large schools in that state? The reports of the State Auditor show that the Negro to-day owns at least one twenty-sixth of the total real estate in that commonwealth exclusive of his holdings in towns and cities, and that in the counties east of the Blue Ridge Mountains he owns one-sixteenth. In Middlesex County he owns one-sixth; in Hanover onefourth. In Georgia, the official records show that, largely through the influence of educated men and women from Atlanta schools and others, the Negroes added last year $1,526,000 to their taxable property, making the total amount upon which they pay taxes in that State alone $16,700,000. From nothing to $16,000,000 in one State in forty years does not seem to prove that education is hurting the race. Relative progress has been made in Alabama and other Southern States. Every man or woman who graduates from the Hampton or Tuskegee Institutes, who has become intelligent and skilled in any one of the industries of the South, is not only in demand at an increased salary on the part of my race, but there is equal demand from the white race. One of the largest manufacturing concerns in Birmingham, Alabama, keeps a standing order at the Tuskegee Institute to the effect that it will employ every man who graduates from our foundry department.

When the South had a wholly ignorant and wholly slave Negro population, she produced about 4,000,000 bales of cotton; now she has a wholly free and partly educated Negro population, and the South produces nearly 10,000,000 bales of cotton, besides more food products than were ever grown in its history. It should not be overlooked that it is not the Negro alone who produces cotton, but it is his labour that produces most of it. And while he may pay a small direct tax, his labour makes it very convenient for others to pay direct taxes.

Judged purely from an economic or industrial standpoint, the education of the Negro is paying, and will pay more largely in the future in proportion as educational opportunities are increased. A careful examination shows that, of the men and women trained at the Hampton and Tuskegee schools, not ten per cent. can be found in idleness at any season of the year.

Years ago some one asked an eminent clergyman in Boston if Christianity is a failure. The Reverend doctor replied that it had never been tried. When people are bold enough to suggest that the education of the Negro is a failure, I reply that it has never been tried. The fact is that 44.5 per cent. of the coloured people of this country to-day are illiterate. A very large proportion of those classed as educated have the merest smattering of knowledge, which means practically no education. Can the Negro child get an education in school four months and out of school eight months? Can the white child of the South who receives $4.92 per capita for education, or the black child who receives $2.21, be said to be given an equal chance in the battle of life, or has education been tried on them? The official records in Louisiana, for instance, show that less than one-fourth of the Negro children of school age attend any school during the year. This one-fourth was in school for a period of less than five months, and each Negro child of school age in the State had spent on him for education last year but $1.89, while each child of school age in the State of New York had spent on him $20.53. In the former slave States ninety per cent. of the Negro children of school age did not attend school for six months during the year 1900.

Wherever the race is given an opportunity for education, it takes advantage of that opportunity, and the change can be seen in the improved material, educational, moral and religious condition of the masses. Contrast two townships, one in Louisiana, where the race has had little chance, with one in Farmville, Virginia, by means of the United States Bulletin of the Department of Labour. In the

Louisiana township only 10 per cent. attend school, and they attend for but four months in a year, and 71 per cent. of the people are illiterate. And as a result of this ignorance and neglect, we find that only 50 per cent. of the people living together as man and wife are legally married. Largely through the leadership of Hampton graduates, 56 per cent. of the black children in Farmville, Virginia, attend either public or private school from six to eight months. There is only 39 per cent. of illiteracy. Practically all the people living together as man and wife are legally married, and in the whole community only 15 per cent. of the births are illegitimate.

But the vital point which I want to emphasise is the disposition of the Negro to exercise self-help in the building up of his own schools in connection with the State public school system. Wherever we send out from Tuskegee, or any of our Southern colleges, a Negro leader of proper character, he shows the people in most cases how to extend the school term beyond the few months provided for by the State. Out of their poverty the Southern States are making a tremendous effort to extend and improve the school term each year, but while this improvement is taking place, the Negro leaders of the character to which I have referred must be depended upon largely to keep alive the spark of education.

It now seems settled that the great body of our people are to reside for all time in the Southern portion of the United States. Since this is true, there is no more helpful and patriotic service than to help cement a friendship between the two races that shall be manly, honourable, and permanent. In this work of moulding and guiding a public sentiment that shall forever maintain peace and good-will between the races on terms commendable to each, it is on the Negro who comes out of our universities, colleges, and industrial schools that we must largely depend. Few people realise how, under the most difficult and trying circumstances, during the last forty years, it has been the educated Negro who counselled patience and self-control and thus averted a war of races. Every Negro going out from our institutions properly educated becomes a link in the chain that shall forever bind the two races together in all the essentials of life.

Finally, reduced to its last analysis, there are but two questions that constitute the problem of this country so far as the black and white races are concerned. The answer to the one rests with my people, the other with the white race. For my race, one of its dangers is that it may grow impatient and feel that it can get upon its feet by artificial and superficial efforts rather than by the slower but surer process which means one step at a time through all the constructive grades of industrial, mental, moral, and social development which all races have had to follow that have become independent and strong.

I would counsel: We must be sure that we shall make our greatest progress by keeping our feet on the earth, and by remembering that an inch of progress is worth a yard of complaint. For the white race, the danger is that in its prosperity and power it may forget the claims of a weaker people; may forget that a strong race, like an individual, should put its hand upon its heart and ask, if it were placed in similar circumstances, how it would like the world to treat it; that the stronger race may forget that, in proportion as it lifts up the poorest and weakest, even by a hair's breadth, it strengthens and ennobles itself.

All the Negro race asks is that the door which rewards industry, thrift, intelligence, and character be left as wide open for him as for the foreigner who constantly comes to our country. More than this, he has no right to request. Less than this, a Republic has no right to vouchsafe.